# Instructor's Test Battery

T H I R D   E D I T I O N

# Essentials of College Mathematics

## FOR BUSINESS, ECONOMICS, LIFE SCIENCES, AND SOCIAL SCIENCES

R A Y M O N D   A.   B A R N E T T
Merritt College

M I C H A E L   R.   Z I E G L E R
Marquette University

Prentice Hall
Upper Saddle River, New Jersey 07458

©2000 by PRENTICE-HALL, INC.
A Pearson Education Company
Upper Saddle River, New Jersey 07458

10  9  8  7  6  5  4  3

ISBN 0-02-305932-X
Printed in the United States of America

# TEST BATTERY
## Description and Use

## Description

This test battery was produced from a computer printout of DellenTest, a computer random generated test system utilizing either IBM compatible or Apple Macintosh computers. The computer-generated test system is also available without charge to any department adopting the text. The test system contains over 320 different problem algorithms directly related to material in the text. These carefully constructed algorithms use random number generators to produce different, yet equivalent, versions of each of these problems. In addition, the Macintosh version incorporates a unique **editing function** that allows the instructor to create additional problems, or alter any of the existing problems in the test, using a full set of mathematical notation. The test system is available now in both **free-response and multiple choice editions.** An almost unlimited number of quizzes, review exercises, chapter tests, mid-terms, and final examinations, each different from the other, can be generated quickly and easily. At the same time, the system will produce answer keys and student work sheets, if desired. See the Preface of ESSENTIALS OF COLLEGE MATHEMATICS, Third Edition for more information about the computer-generated test system.

## Use

The test battery consists of three iterations of all the questions available for the text, organized by chapter and identified by Form A-A, Form A-B, and Form A-C. Answers for each form are included, but student worksheets are not. It is not recommended that all problems available for a chapter be used in a single test — generally, there are more problems for each chapter than most students will be able to finish in a 50-minute period. Select problem types and levels of difficulty to tailor the test to your own objectives and time constraints.

Essentials of College Mathematics, Third Edition
Raymond A. Barnett and Michael R. Ziegler

## CHAPTER 1    Basic Algebraic Operations

1.  One of the following is false; indicate by letter which one:
    (A) $9 \notin \{5, 6, 7, 8\}$          (B) $\{6\} \subset \{5, 6, 7, 8\}$
    (C) $6 \in \{5, 6, 7, 8\}$          (D) $6 \subset \{5, 6, 7, 8\}$

2.  Given the universal set $U = \{4, 5, 6, 7, 8, 9\}$ and the subsets
    $M = \{4, 6, 7, 9\}$ and $N = \{5, 6, 7\}$, find $M' \cap N$.

3.  In a marketing survey involving 1,000 randomly chosen people, it is
    found that 720 use brand P, 480 use brand Q, and 240 use both brands.
    How many people in the survey use neither brand P nor brand Q?

4.  Let N be the set of natural numbers, Z the set of integers, Q the
    set of rational numbers, and R the set of real numbers. Indicate
    to which sets each of the following belong:

    A) $\frac{3}{5}$     B) 10     C) $-45$     D) $\sqrt{2}$

5.  Graph and label the points with the following coordinates on the
    number line below.

    $A = -\frac{10}{3}$       $B = 3.8$       $C = \sqrt{2}$

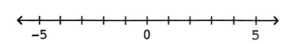

6.  Indicate True or False; for each false statement, give real number
    replacements to illustrate its falseness.

    I)   $(a \cdot b) \cdot c = a \cdot (b \cdot c)$

    II)  $a \cdot b = b \cdot a$

    III) $a - b = b - a$

    IV)  $(a - b) - c = a - (b - c)$

7.  Perform the operations and simplify:

    $4(2x^4 - 4x^3 + 1) + x^6(4x^4 - 9) + 4[x^6 - (2x^3 + 4)]$

8.  Multiply:

    $(4x - 3)(3x + 1)$

9.  Perform the operations and simplify:

    $(6m + 3n)(6m - 3n) + 3(m + 5n)^2$

## CHAPTER 1    Basic Algebraic Operations

10. Factor out all common factors, relative to the integers.

    $3x^5y^3 - 12x^4y^4 - 15x^3y^5$

11. Factor out all common factors, relative to the integers.

    $2x(3x + 7) - 5(3x + 7)$

12. Which polynomial can be factored using integer coefficients?  Find its factored form.

    I)  $12x^2 - 19x - 21$

    II)  $16m^2 + 9n^2$

    III)  $x^2 + 7x - 3$

13. Factor using integer coefficients.

    $16x^5y^2 - 24x^5y + 9x^5$

14. Reduce the rational expression to lowest terms.

    $$\frac{x^3 - 25x}{4x^3 - 17x^2 - 15x}$$

15. Perform the indicated operation and reduce to lowest terms.

    $$\frac{30x^3y}{2xy + 14y} \cdot \frac{x^2 - 49}{4x^2 - 28x}$$

16. Perform the indicated operation and reduce to lowest terms.

    $$\frac{3x + 3y}{x^2 - 2xy - 8y^2} \div \frac{21x + 21y}{x^2 + 6xy + 8y^2}$$

17. Combine into a single fraction and simplify.

    $$\frac{1}{9x^5} - \frac{3x + 1}{7x^4} + \frac{7}{63x}$$

18. Combine into a single fraction and simplify.

    $$\frac{y - 6}{y^2 - 1} - \frac{y + 6}{y^2 - 2y + 1} - \frac{5}{1 - y}$$

19. Express as a simple fraction reduced to lowest terms.

    $$\frac{\frac{a}{b} - 3 + \frac{2b}{a}}{\frac{a}{b} - 1 - \frac{2b}{a}}$$

CHAPTER 1    Basic Algebraic Operations

20. Simplify and express answer using positive exponents.

$x^8 x^{-9}$

21. Simplify and express answer using positive exponents.

$(u^2 v^{-3})^{-6}$

22. Change to simplest radical form.

$$\frac{2 + 3\sqrt{y}}{9 - \sqrt{y}}$$

23. Change to simplest radical form.

$\sqrt{36m^8 n^8} \sqrt{4m^8 n^2}$

24. Change the rational form to simplest radical form.

$(2x^2 y^5 z^{42})^{3/7}$

25. Simplify and express the answer using positive exponents only.

$(2x^{-2/3} y^{1/3})^3$

26. Change to simplest radical form.

$$\frac{36x^7 y}{\sqrt{6x}}$$

27. Write in simplest radical form.

$\sqrt[5]{243x^{23} y^{17}}$

## Key Sheet — CHAPTER 1

[1]  (D)

[2]  {5}

[3]  40

[4]  (A) Q, R    (B) N, Z, Q, R    (C) Z, Q, R   (D) R

[5]

[6]  I) True    II) True    III) False   IV) False

[7]  $4x^{10} - 5x^6 + 8x^4 - 24x^3 - 12$

[8]  $12x^2 - 5x - 3$

[9]  $39m^2 + 30mn + 66n^2$

[10]  $3x^3y^3(x^2 - 4xy - 5y^2)$

[11]  $(3x + 7)(2x - 5)$

[12]  I; $(4x + 3)(3x - 7)$

[13]  $x^5(4y - 3)^2$

[14]  $\dfrac{x + 5}{4x + 3}$

[15]  $\dfrac{15x^2}{4}$

[16]  $\dfrac{x + 4y}{7(x - 4y)}$

[17]  $\dfrac{7 - 9x - 27x^2 + 7x^4}{63x^5}$

[18]  $\dfrac{5y^2 - 14y - 5}{(y + 1)(y - 1)^2}$

Key Sheet - CHAPTER 1

[19] $\dfrac{a - b}{a + b}$

[20] $\dfrac{1}{x}$

[21] $\dfrac{v^{18}}{u^{12}}$

[22] $\dfrac{18 + 29\sqrt{y} + 3y}{81 - y}$

[23] $12m^8 n^5$

[24] $y^2 z^{18} \; \sqrt[7]{8x^6 y}$

[25] $\dfrac{8y}{x^2}$

[26] $6x^6 y \; \sqrt{6x}$

[27] $3x^4 y^3 \; \sqrt[5]{x^3 y^2}$

Essentials of College Mathematics, Third Edition
Raymond A. Barnett and Michael R. Ziegler

CHAPTER 1    Basic Algebraic Operations

1.  One of the following is false; indicate by letter which one:
    (A) $6 \notin \{2, 3, 4, 5\}$      (B) $2 \in \{2, 3, 4, 5\}$
    (C) $\{2\} \subset \{2, 3, 4, 5\}$      (D) $2 \subset \{2, 3, 4, 5\}$

2.  Given the universal set $U = \{0, 1, 2, 3, 4, 5\}$ and the subsets
    $M = \{0, 2, 3, 5\}$ and $N = \{1, 2, 3\}$, find $M' \cap N$.

3.  In a marketing survey involving 1,000 randomly chosen people, it is
    found that 630 use brand P, 420 use brand Q, and 210 use both brands.
    How many people in the survey use neither brand P nor brand Q?

4.  Let N be the set of natural numbers, Z the set of integers, Q the
    set of rational numbers, and R the set of real numbers.  Indicate
    to which sets each of the following belong:

    A) -93    B) 51    C) 2.7182...    D) 3.14

5.  Graph and label the points with the following coordinates on the
    number line below.

    $A = \frac{1}{3}$      $B = -1.2$      $C = \sqrt{2}$

    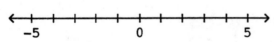

6.  Indicate True or False; for each false statement, give real number
    replacements to illustrate its falseness.

    I)   $a - b = b - a$

    II)  $(a \cdot b) \cdot c = a \cdot (b \cdot c)$

    III) $(a \div b) \div c = a \div (b \div c)$

    IV)  $a + b = b + a$

7.  Perform the operations and simplify:

    $3(2x^3 - 3x^2 + 7) + x^4(3x^3 - 8) + 3[x^4 - (2x^2 + 3)]$

8.  Multiply:

    $(3x - 1)(4x + 3)$

9.  Perform the operations and simplify:

    $(2m + 5n)(2m - 5n) + 5(m + 4n)^2$

---

CHAPTER 1     Basic Algebraic Operations

---

10. Factor out all common factors, relative to the integers.

    $2x^3y - 10x^5y^5 - 6x^2y^3$

11. Factor out all common factors, relative to the integers.

    $3x(2x + 5) - 7(2x + 5)$

12. Which polynomial can be factored using integer coefficients?  Find its factored form.

    I)  $x^2 + 8x - 5$

    II)  $4m^2 + 25n^2$

    III)  $6x^2 - x - 40$

13. Factor using integer coefficients.

    $25x^4y^2 - 20x^4y + 4x^4$

14. Reduce the rational expression to lowest terms.

    $$\frac{x^3 - 49x}{5x^3 - 32x^2 - 21x}$$

15. Perform the indicated operation and reduce to lowest terms.

    $$\frac{30x^3y}{4xy + 16y} \cdot \frac{x^2 - 16}{4x^2 - 16x}$$

16. Perform the indicated operation and reduce to lowest terms.

    $$\frac{3x + 3y}{x^2 - 7xy - 18y^2} \div \frac{15x + 15y}{x^2 + 11xy + 18y^2}$$

17. Combine into a single fraction and simplify.

    $$\frac{1}{25x^6} - \frac{5x + 1}{3x^5} + \frac{3}{75x}$$

18. Combine into a single fraction and simplify.

    $$\frac{y - 8}{y^2 - 9} - \frac{y + 8}{y^2 - 6y + 9} - \frac{1}{3 - y}$$

19. Express as a simple fraction reduced to lowest terms.

    $$\frac{\frac{a}{b} - 1 - \frac{2b}{a}}{\frac{a}{b} - 3 + \frac{2b}{a}}$$

## CHAPTER 1    Basic Algebraic Operations

20.  Simplify and express answer using positive exponents.

$x^2 x^{-6}$

21.  Simplify and express answer using positive exponents.

$(u^4 v^{-6})^{-2}$

22.  Change to simplest radical form.

$$\frac{3 + 2\sqrt{y}}{3 - \sqrt{y}}$$

23.  Change to simplest radical form.

$\sqrt{48m^6 n^6} \ \sqrt{3m^6 n^2}$

24.  Change the rational form to simplest radical form.

$(2xy^6 z^{21})^{2/7}$

25.  Simplify and express the answer using positive exponents only.

$(2x^{-4/5} y^{2/5})^5$

26.  Change to simplest radical form.

$$\frac{x^8 y}{\sqrt{x}}$$

27.  Write in simplest radical form.

$\sqrt[3]{8x^5 y^7}$

## Key Sheet - CHAPTER 1

[1]  (D)

[2]  {1}

[3]  160

[4]  (A) Z, Q, R    (B) N, Z, Q, R    (C) R   (D) Q, R

[5]

[6]  I) False    II) True    III) False    IV) True

[7]  $3x^7 - 5x^4 + 6x^3 - 15x^2 + 12$

[8]  $12x^2 + 5x - 3$

[9]  $9m^2 + 40mn + 55n^2$

[10] $2x^2y(x - 5x^3y^4 - 3y^2)$

[11] $(2x + 5)(3x - 7)$

[12] III; $(2x + 5)(3x - 8)$

[13] $x^4(5y - 2)^2$

[14] $\dfrac{x + 7}{5x + 3}$

[15] $\dfrac{15x^2}{8}$

[16] $\dfrac{x + 9y}{5(x - 9y)}$

[17] $\dfrac{3 - 25x - 125x^2 + 3x^5}{75x^6}$

[18] $\dfrac{y^2 - 22y - 9}{(y + 3)(y - 3)^2}$

## Key Sheet – CHAPTER 1

[19] $\dfrac{a + b}{a - b}$

[20] $\dfrac{1}{x^4}$

[21] $\dfrac{v^{12}}{u^8}$

[22] $\dfrac{9 + 9\sqrt{y} + 2y}{9 - y}$

[23] $12m^6 n^4$

[24] $yz^6 \; \sqrt[7]{4x^2 y^5}$

[25] $\dfrac{32y^2}{x^4}$

[26] $x^7 y \; \sqrt{x}$

[27] $2xy^2 \; \sqrt[3]{x^2 y}$

Essentials of College Mathematics, Third Edition
Raymond A. Barnett and Michael R. Ziegler

## CHAPTER 1    Basic Algebraic Operations

1.  One of the following is false; indicate by letter which one:
    (A) $\{1\} \subset \{1, 2, 3, 4\}$       (B) $1 \in \{1, 2, 3, 4\}$
    (C) $1 \subset \{1, 2, 3, 4\}$       (D) $5 \notin \{1, 2, 3, 4\}$

2.  Given the universal set $U = \{1, 2, 3, 4, 5, 6\}$ and the subsets
    $M = \{1, 3, 4, 6\}$ and $N = \{2, 3, 4\}$, find $M \cup N'$.

3.  In a marketing survey involving 1,000 randomly chosen people, it is
    found that 750 use brand P, 500 use brand Q, and 250 use both brands.
    How many people in the survey use either brand P or brand Q?

4.  Let N be the set of natural numbers, Z the set of integers, Q the
    set of rational numbers, and R the set of real numbers.  Indicate
    to which sets each of the following belong:

    A) -87    B) $.6\overline{6}$    C) $\sqrt[5]{7}$    D) 52

5.  Graph and label the points with the following coordinates on the
    number line below.

    $A = \dfrac{3}{4}$       $B = -1.2$       $C = \pi$

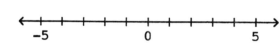

6.  Indicate True or False; for each false statement, give real number
    replacements to illustrate its falseness.

    I)   $a - b = b - a$

    II)  $(a - b) - c = a - (b - c)$

    III) $a \cdot b = b \cdot a$

    IV)  $(a \cdot b) \cdot c = a \cdot (b \cdot c)$

7.  Perform the operations and simplify:

    $2(4x^5 - 2x^4 + 9) + x^7(2x^5 - 8) + 2[x^7 - (4x^4 + 2)]$

8.  Multiply:

    $(2x - 2)(3x + 3)$

9.  Perform the operations and simplify:

    $(4m + 5n)(4m - 5n) + 5(m + 6n)^2$

## CHAPTER 1    Basic Algebraic Operations

10.  Factor out all common factors, relative to the integers.

$$x^4y^3 - 4x^4y^4 - 4xy^4$$

11.  Factor out all common factors, relative to the integers.

$$4x(3x + 8) - 5(3x + 8)$$

12.  Which polynomial can be factored using integer coefficients?  Find its factored form.

I)   $16m^2 + 9n^2$

II)  $x^2 + 7x - 3$

III) $12x^2 - 19x - 21$

13.  Factor using integer coefficients.

$$4x^3y^2 - 4x^3y + x^3$$

14.  Reduce the rational expression to lowest terms.

$$\frac{x^3 - 9x}{4x^3 - 11x^2 - 3x}$$

15.  Perform the indicated operation and reduce to lowest terms.

$$\frac{105x^3y}{2xy + 4y} \cdot \frac{x^2 - 4}{49x^2 - 98x}$$

16.  Perform the indicated operation and reduce to lowest terms.

$$\frac{3x + 3y}{x^2 - 5xy - 14y^2} \div \frac{6x + 6y}{x^2 + 9xy + 14y^2}$$

17.  Combine into a single fraction and simplify.

$$\frac{1}{49x^6} - \frac{7x + 1}{5x^5} + \frac{5}{245x}$$

18.  Combine into a single fraction and simplify.

$$\frac{y - 4}{y^2 - 1} - \frac{y + 4}{y^2 - 2y + 1} - \frac{3}{1 - y}$$

19.  Express as a simple fraction reduced to lowest terms.

$$\frac{\frac{a}{b} + 3 + \frac{2b}{a}}{\frac{a}{b} - \frac{4b}{a}}$$

## CHAPTER 1    Basic Algebraic Operations

20. Simplify and express answer using positive exponents.

$x^6 x^{-8}$

21. Simplify and express answer using positive exponents.

$(u^5 v^{-4})^{-6}$

22. Change to simplest radical form.

$$\frac{4 + 2\sqrt{y}}{9 - \sqrt{y}}$$

23. Change to simplest radical form.

$\sqrt{32m^8 n^4} \ \sqrt{2m^8 n^2}$

24. Change the rational form to simplest radical form.

$(2xy^6 z^{28})^{2/7}$

25. Simplify and express the answer using positive exponents only.

$(2x^{-2/3} y^{1/3})^6$

26. Change to simplest radical form.

$$\frac{9x^7 y}{\sqrt{3x}}$$

27. Write in simplest radical form.

$\sqrt[3]{8x^{10} y^5}$

## Key Sheet - CHAPTER 1

[1]  (C)

[2]  {1, 3, 4, 5, 6}

[3]  1000

[4]  (A) Z, Q, R    (B) Q, R    (C) R    (D) N, Z, Q, R

[5]  

[6]  I) False    II) False    III) True    IV) True

[7]  $2x^{12} - 6x^7 + 8x^5 - 12x^4 + 14$

[8]  $6x^2 - 6$

[9]  $21m^2 + 60mn + 155n^2$

[10]  $xy^3(x^3 - 4x^3y - 4y)$

[11]  $(3x + 8)(4x - 5)$

[12]  III; $(4x + 3)(3x - 7)$

[13]  $x^3(2y - 1)^2$

[14]  $\dfrac{x + 3}{4x + 1}$

[15]  $\dfrac{15x^2}{14}$

[16]  $\dfrac{x + 7y}{2(x - 7y)}$

[17]  $\dfrac{5 - 49x - 343x^2 + 5x^5}{245x^6}$

[18]  $\dfrac{3y^2 - 10y - 3}{(y + 1)(y - 1)^2}$

Key Sheet - CHAPTER 1

[19] $\dfrac{a + b}{a - 2b}$

[20] $\dfrac{1}{x^2}$

[21] $\dfrac{v^{24}}{u^{30}}$

[22] $\dfrac{36 + 22\sqrt{y} + 2y}{81 - y}$

[23] $8m^8n^3$

[24] $yz^8 \sqrt[7]{4x^2y^5}$

[25] $\dfrac{64y^2}{x^4}$

[26] $3x^6y \sqrt{3x}$

[27] $2x^3y \sqrt[3]{xy^2}$

Essentials of College Mathematics, Third Edition
Raymond A. Barnett and Michael R. Ziegler

CHAPTER 2     Equations, Graphs, and Functions

1.   Solve: $\dfrac{x - 5}{24} - \dfrac{x - 4}{48} = \dfrac{3 - x}{16} - 5$

2.   Solve and graph on a real number line:  $4(x + 4) > 6(x - 5) + 6$

3.   Solve and graph on a real number line:  $-7 < \dfrac{2}{3}x - 3 \le 5$

4.   You have $50,000 and wish to invest part at 10% and the rest at 6%. How much should be invested at each rate to produce the same return as if it all had been invested at 7%?

5.   Solve: $2z^2 = 8z$

6.   Solve and leave the answer in radical form: $2z^2 = 4z + 1$

7.   Factor, if possible, as the product of two first-degree polynomials with integer coefficients.
     $4x^2 - 101x + 357$

8.   If P dollars is invested at 100r% compounded annually, at the end of 2 years it will grow to $A = P(1 + r)^2$.  At what interest rate will $10,000 grow to $11,400 in 2 years?  (Compute 100r% to two decimal places.)

9.   The supply and demand equations for a certain product are
     $s = 1,000p - 2,500$ and $d = \dfrac{1,500}{p}$
     where p is the price in dollars.  Find the price where supply equals demand.

10.  Graph $3x + 5y = 30$ in a rectangular coordinate system.  What is the slope of the graph?

11.  Write the equation of a line that passes through $(-4, 5)$ and $(2, -3)$. Write the final answer in the form $Ax + By = C$ where A, B and C are integers with no common divisors (other than $\pm 1$) and $A > 0$.

12.  A small company that makes hand-sewn leather shoes has fixed costs of $280 a day, and total costs of $1400 per day at an output of 20 pairs of shoes per day.  Assume that total cost C is linearly related to output x.  Find an equation of the line relating output to cost.  Write the final answer in the form $C = mx + b$.

---

CHAPTER 2    Equations, Graphs, and Functions

---

13. Only one of the following functions has domain which is not equal to all real numbers.  State which function and state its domain.

    (A) $f(x) = \dfrac{2x}{5 - x}$

    (B) $g(x) = \dfrac{x + 7}{2}$

    (C) $h(x) = 4x^2 - 3x - 5$

14. For $f(t) = 2t + 4$ and $g(t) = 1 - t^2$, find $3f(2) - g(-2) + g(0)$.

15. For $f(s) = 2 - 2s$, find $\dfrac{f(a + h) - f(a)}{h}$.

16. A dance studio charges \$60 per student for a series of four 2-hour dance lessons.  The studio's costs are \$15 per hour for the instructor, \$20 per lesson for room rental, and \$5 per student for miscellaneous expenses.  If x is the number of students enrolled in the class, express the studio's profit P(x) in terms of x.  Find the profit if 10 students enroll in the class.

17. Graph the linear function defined by
    $f(x) = -\dfrac{1}{3}x - 2$
    and indicate the slope and intercepts.

18. Graph $f(x) = -x^2 - 4x - 4$ and indicate the maximum or minimum value of $f(x)$, whichever exists.

19. Graph the following function.  State its domain and range.
    $$f(x) = \begin{cases} 1 & -6 \leq x \leq 0 \\ x + 1 & 0 < x \leq 6 \end{cases}$$

20. A piece of equipment was purchased by a company for \$60,000 and is assumed to have a salvage value of \$18,000 in 10 years.  If its value is depreciated linearly from \$60,000 to \$18,000, find a linear function in the form $V(t) = mt + b$, t time in years, that will give the salvage value at any time t, $0 \leq t \leq 10$.

Key Sheet - CHAPTER 2

[1]  $x = -\dfrac{225}{4}$

[2]  $x < 20$ or $(-\infty, 20)$

[3]  $-6 < x \leq 12$ or $(-6, 12]$

[4]  $12,500 at 10%
     $37,500 at 6%

[5]  $z = 0$ or $4$

[6]  $z = \dfrac{2 \pm \sqrt{6}}{2}$

[7]  $(4x - 17)(x - 21)$

[8]  6.77%

[9]  $3

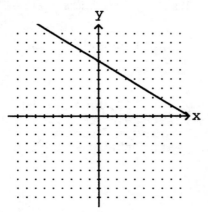

[10]  Slope $= -\dfrac{3}{5}$

[11]  $4x + 3y = -1$

[12]  $C = 56x + 280$

Key Sheet - CHAPTER 2

[13] $f(x) = \dfrac{2x}{5 - x}$ has domain all real numbers except x = 5

[14] 28

[15] -2

[16] P(x) = 55x - 200, P(10) = $350

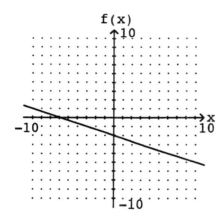

x intercept = -6   y intercept = -2

[17] slope = $-\dfrac{1}{3}$

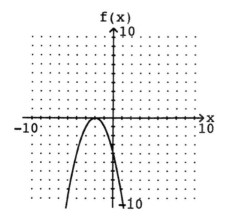

[18] Max f(x) = 0

Key Sheet – CHAPTER 2

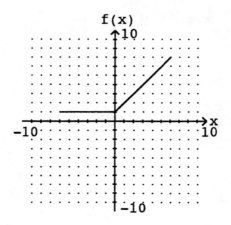

[19] domain:  [-6, 6]    range: [1, 7]

[20] V(t) = -4,200t + 60,000

Essentials of College Mathematics, Third Edition
Raymond A. Barnett and Michael R. Ziegler

CHAPTER 2     Equations, Graphs, and Functions

1.   Solve: $\dfrac{x-5}{6} - \dfrac{x-3}{12} = \dfrac{5-x}{4} - 4$

2.   Solve and graph on a real number line:  $2(x + 4) \leq 4(x - 5) - 4$

3.   Solve and graph on a real number line:  $-9 \leq \frac{2}{7}x - 1 < 5$

4.   You have $30,000 and wish to invest part at 11% and the rest at 6%. How much should be invested at each rate to produce the same return as if it all had been invested at 8%?

5.   Solve: $6z^2 = 6z$

6.   Solve and leave the answer in radical form: $4z^2 = 2z + 1$

7.   Factor, if possible, as the product of two first-degree polynomials with integer coefficients.
     $4x^2 - 119x + 390$

8.   If P dollars is invested at 100r% compounded annually, at the end of 2 years it will grow to $A = P(1 + r)^2$. At what interest rate will $1,000 grow to $1,320 in 2 years?  (Compute 100r% to two decimal places.)

9.   The supply and demand equations for a certain product are
     $s = 1,500p - 5,500$ and $d = \dfrac{2,000}{p}$
     where p is the price in dollars.  Find the price where supply equals demand.

10.  Graph $3x - 5y = 30$ in a rectangular coordinate system.  What is the slope of the graph?

11.  Write the equation of a line that passes through $(-5, 1)$ and $(2, -1)$. Write the final answer in the form $Ax + By = C$ where A, B and C are integers with no common divisors (other than ±1) and $A > 0$.

12.  A small company that makes hand-sewn leather shoes has fixed costs of $340 a day, and total costs of $1300 per day at an output of 20 pairs of shoes per day.  Assume that total cost C is linearly related to output x.  Find an equation of the line relating output to cost.  Write the final answer in the form $C = mx + b$.

## CHAPTER 2    Equations, Graphs, and Functions

13. Only one of the following functions has domain which is not equal to all real numbers. State which function and state its domain.

    (A) $g(x) = \dfrac{x + 7}{2}$

    (B) $f(x) = \dfrac{2x}{21 - x}$

    (C) $h(x) = 4x^2 - 3x - 5$

14. For $f(t) = -3t + 4$ and $g(t) = 2 - t^2$, find $5f(3) - g(-3) + g(0)$.

15. For $f(u) = 5 - 2u$, find $\dfrac{f(a + h) - f(a)}{h}$.

16. A dance studio charges $50 per student for a series of four 2-hour dance lessons. The studio's costs are $15 per hour for the instructor, $20 per lesson for room rental, and $5 per student for miscellaneous expenses. If x is the number of students enrolled in the class, express the studio's profit $P(x)$ in terms of x. Find the profit if 10 students enroll in the class.

17. Graph the linear function defined by
    $$f(x) = \tfrac{1}{2}x - 1$$
    and indicate the slope and intercepts.

18. Graph $f(x) = x^2 - 4x + 4$ and indicate the maximum or minimum value of $f(x)$, whichever exists.

19. Graph the following function. State its domain and range.
    $$f(x) = \begin{cases} -2 & -6 \le x \le 1 \\ x - 3 & 1 < x \le 6 \end{cases}$$

20. A piece of equipment was purchased by a company for $20,000 and is assumed to have a salvage value of $6,000 in 20 years. If its value is depreciated linearly from $20,000 to $6,000, find a linear function in the form $V(t) = mt + b$, t time in years, that will give the salvage value at any time t, $0 \le t \le 20$.

[1]   $x = -\dfrac{13}{2}$

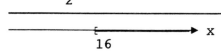

[2]   $x \geq 16$ or $[16, \infty)$

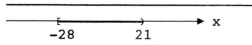

[3]   $-28 \leq x < 21$ or $[-28, 21)$

[4]   $12,000 at 11%
      $18,000 at 6%

[5]   $z = 0$ or $1$

[6]   $z = \dfrac{1 \pm \sqrt{5}}{4}$

[7]   $(4x - 15)(x - 26)$

[8]   14.89%

[9]   $4

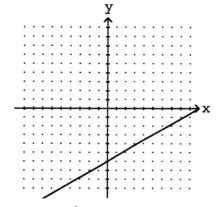

[10]  Slope $= \dfrac{3}{5}$

[11]  $2x + 7y = -3$

[12]  $C = 48x + 340$

Key Sheet - CHAPTER 2

[13] $f(x) = \dfrac{2x}{21 - x}$ has domain all real numbers except x = 21

[14] −16

[15] −2

[16] P(x) = 45x − 200, P(10) = $250

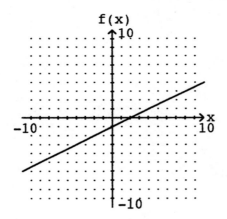

[17] x intercept = 2   y intercept = −1
slope = $\dfrac{1}{2}$

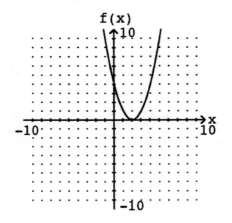

[18] Min f(x) = 0

Key Sheet - CHAPTER 2

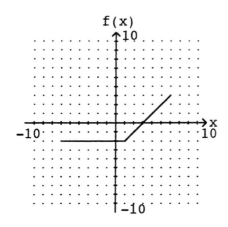

[19] domain:  [-6, 6]    range: [-2, 3]

[20] V(t) = -700t + 20,000

## CHAPTER 2     Equations, Graphs, and Functions

1. Solve: $\dfrac{x-3}{24} - \dfrac{x-3}{48} = \dfrac{4-x}{16} - 5$

2. Solve and graph on a real number line: $4(x+6) < 6(x+1) + 4$

3. Solve and graph on a real number line: $-5 < \dfrac{2}{7}x + 3 \le 5$

4. You have $10,000 and wish to invest part at 12% and the rest at 8%. How much should be invested at each rate to produce the same return as if it all had been invested at 9%?

5. Solve: $10u^2 = 2u$

6. Solve and leave the answer in radical form: $6u^2 = 6u + 1$

7. Factor, if possible, as the product of two first-degree polynomials with integer coefficients.
$2x^2 - 63x + 418$

8. If P dollars is invested at 100r% compounded annually, at the end of 2 years it will grow to $A = P(1 + r)^2$. At what interest rate will $100 grow to $130 in 2 years? (Compute 100r% to two decimal places.)

9. The supply and demand equations for a certain product are
$s = 1,000p - 3,500$ and $d = \dfrac{7,500}{p}$
where p is the price in dollars. Find the price where supply equals demand.

10. Graph $3x + 2y = 12$ in a rectangular coordinate system. What is the slope of the graph?

11. Write the equation of a line that passes through (-3, 4) and (1, -2). Write the final answer in the form $Ax + By = C$ where A, B and C are integers with no common divisors (other than ±1) and A > 0.

12. A small company that makes hand-sewn leather shoes has fixed costs of $300 a day, and total costs of $900 per day at an output of 20 pairs of shoes per day. Assume that total cost C is linearly related to output x. Find an equation of the line relating output to cost. Write the final answer in the form $C = mx + b$.

---

### CHAPTER 2    Equations, Graphs, and Functions

---

13. Only one of the following functions has domain which is not equal to all real numbers.  State which function and state its domain.

    (A) $h(x) = 4x^2 - 3x - 5$

    (B) $g(x) = \dfrac{x + 7}{2}$

    (C) $f(x) = \dfrac{2x}{47 - x}$

14. For $f(t) = 5t - 2$ and $g(t) = 3 - t^2$, find $f(3) - g(-3) + g(0)$.

15. For $f(x) = 5 - 3x$, find $\dfrac{f(a + h) - f(a)}{h}$.

16. A dance studio charges $80 per student for a series of four 2-hour dance lessons.  The studio's costs are $20 per hour for the instructor, $15 per lesson for room rental, and $4 per student for miscellaneous expenses.  If x is the number of students enrolled in the class, express the studio's profit P(x) in terms of x.  Find the profit if 10 students enroll in the class.

17. Graph the linear function defined by
    $$f(x) = -\tfrac{1}{2}x + 3$$
    and indicate the slope and intercepts.

18. Graph $f(x) = -x^2 + 4$ and indicate the maximum or minimum value of f(x), whichever exists.

19. Graph the following function.  State its domain and range.
    $$f(x) = \begin{cases} -3 & -7 \le x \le 2 \\ -x - 1 & 2 < x \le 7 \end{cases}$$

20. A piece of equipment was purchased by a company for $90,000 and is assumed to have a salvage value of $27,000 in 10 years.  If its value is depreciated linearly from $90,000 to $27,000, find a linear function in the form V(t) = mt + b, t time in years, that will give the salvage value at any time t, $0 \le t \le 10$.

## Key Sheet - CHAPTER 2

[1]  $x = -\dfrac{225}{4}$

$$\xrightarrow{\hspace{3cm}} x$$
$$\underset{7}{}$$

[2]  $x > 7$ or $(7, \infty)$

$$\xrightarrow{\hspace{3cm}} x$$
$$\underset{-28 \qquad 7}{}$$

[3]  $-28 < x \leq 7$ or $(-28, 7]$

[4]  $2,500 at 12%
     $7,500 at 8%

[5]  $u = 0$ or $\dfrac{1}{5}$

[6]  $u = \dfrac{3 \pm \sqrt{15}}{6}$

[7]  $(2x - 19)(x - 22)$

[8]  14.02%

[9]  $5

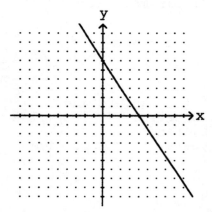

[10]  Slope $= -\dfrac{3}{2}$

[11]  $3x + 2y = -1$

[12]  $C = 30x + 300$

Key Sheet - CHAPTER 2

[13]  $f(x) = \dfrac{2x}{47 - x}$ has domain all real numbers except x = 47

[14]  22

[15]  -3

[16]  P(x) = 76x - 220,  P(10) = $540

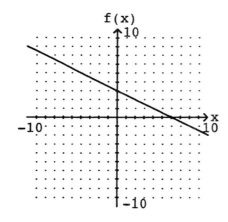

[17]  x intercept = 6   y intercept = 3
slope = $-\dfrac{1}{2}$

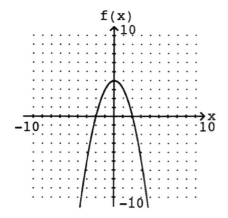

[18]  Max f(x) = 4

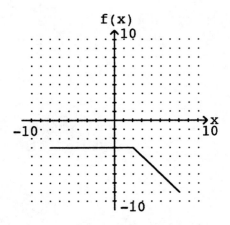

[19] domain:  [-7, 7]    range: [-8, -3]

[20] V(t) = -6,300t + 90,000

# DellenTest MAC 2.0

Copyright © 1995 by Prentice-Hall, Inc.

Essentials of College Mathematics, Third Edition
Raymond A. Barnett and Michael R. Ziegler

CHAPTER 3    Exponential and Logarithmic Functions

1.  Simplify: $\dfrac{3^{2x+3}}{3^{3-2x}}$

2.  Simplify: $\left(\dfrac{3^x}{2^{3y}}\right)^{5x}$

3.  Graph $y = 2^{x+1} - 3$ over the interval $[-4, 2]$.

4.  Solve for x: $3^{4x} = 9^{x-2}$

5.  A particular bacterium is found to have a doubling time of 50 minutes. If a laboratory culture begins with a population of 300 of this bacteria and there is no change in the growth rate, how many bacteria will be present in 145 minutes?

6.  Graph $y = 7e^{-x/4}$, $-2 \le x \le 2$, using a calculator. Choose horizontal and vertical scales as follows:

    Horizontal scale: 1 unit = 5 squares;
    Vertical scale: 1 unit = 1/2 square

7.  Graph $y = 4e^{-0.4x} - 2$ over $[0, 10]$.

8.  Simplify: $e^{6x}(e^x - e^{-4x}) + (4e^x + e^{-x})^2$

9.  If you invest $2,000 in an account paying 7.6% compounded continuously, how much money will be in the account after 14 years?

10. Rewrite in equivalent exponential form: $\log_{16}4 = \dfrac{1}{2}$

11. Rewrite in equivalent logarithmic form: $2^6 = 64$

12. Evaluate: $\log_4 4^{-9}$

13. Solve for x without using a calculator or table:
    $\log_b x - \log_b 4 = \log_b 3 - \log_b(x - 1)$

14. Solve for x:  $\log_4 x + \log_4(x - 6) = \log_4 16$

15. Use a calculator to evaluate: (A) $\log 0.29$    (B) $\ln 1657$

CHAPTER 3    Exponential and Logarithmic Functions

16.    Use a calculator to evaluate $\log_4 22.3$ to four decimal places.

17.    Solve for x to two decimal places (using a calculator):
       $400 = 200(1.03)^x$

18.    If $7,000 is invested at 14% compounded annually, how long will it
       take for it to grow to $9,000, assuming no withdrawals are made?
       Compute answer to the next higher year if not exact. $[A = P(1 + r)^t]$

19.    A country has a population growth rate of 2.6% compounded
       continuously.  At this rate, how long will it take for the
       population of the country to double?

20.    A carbon-14 dating test is performed on a fossil bone, and analysis
       finds that 17% of the original amount of $^{14}C$ is still present
       in the bone.  Estimate the age of the fossil bone.
       (Recall that $^{14}C$ decays according to the equation $A = A_0 e^{-0.000124t}$.)

Key Sheet – CHAPTER 3

[1] $3^{4x}$

[2] $\dfrac{3^{5x^2}}{2^{15xy}}$

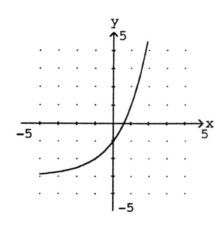

[3]

[4] $x = -2$

[5] 2,239 bacteria

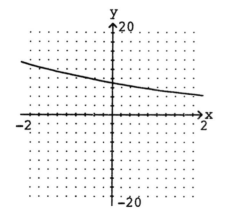

[6]

Key Sheet - CHAPTER 3

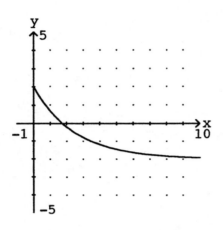

[7]

[8]  $e^{7x} + 15e^{2x} + 8 + e^{-2x}$

[9]  $5,795.88

[10] $4 = 16^{1/2}$

[11] $\log_2 64 = 6$

[12] -9

[13] x = 4

[14] x = 8

[15] (A) log 0.29 = -0.5376    (B) ln 1657 = 7.4128

[16] 2.2395

[17] x = 23.45

[18] 2 years

[19] t = 26.7 years

[20] t ≈ 14,290 years

Essentials of College Mathematics, Third Edition
Raymond A. Barnett and Michael R. Ziegler

Form A-B                                                    Page 1

CHAPTER 3    Exponential and Logarithmic Functions

1.   Simplify: $\dfrac{7^{2x+6}}{7^{6-4x}}$

2.   Simplify: $\left(\dfrac{3^{3x}}{2^{2y}}\right)^{2x}$

3.   Graph $y = 3^{x-3} - 5$ over the interval $[1, 5]$.

4.   Solve for x: $3^{2x} = 27^{x-1}$

5.   A particular bacterium is found to have a doubling time of 20
     minutes.  If a laboratory culture begins with a population of 700 of
     this bacteria and there is no change in the growth rate, how many
     bacteria will be present in 75 minutes?

6.   Graph $y = 5e^{x/2}$, $-2 \le x \le 2$, using a calculator.  Choose
     horizontal and vertical scales as follows:

     Horizontal scale: 1 unit = 5 squares;
     Vertical scale: 1 unit = 1/2 square

7.   Graph $y = 6e^{-0.4x} - 3$ over $[0, 10]$.

8.   Simplify: $e^{5x}(e^x - e^{-3x}) + (e^x + 3e^{-x})^2$

9.   If you invest \$2,000 in an account paying 8.6% compounded
     continuously, how much money will be in the account after 2.5 years?

10.  Rewrite in equivalent exponential form: $\log_9 27 = \dfrac{3}{2}$

11.  Rewrite in equivalent logarithmic form: $4^2 = 16$

12.  Evaluate: $\log_2 2^3$

13.  Solve for x without using a calculator or table:
     $\log_b x - \log_b 2 = \log_b 5 - \log_b(x + 3)$

14.  Solve for x:  $\log_2 x + \log_2(x + 2) = \log_2 24$

15.  Use a calculator to evaluate: (A) $\log 0.35$    (B) $\ln 47$

CHAPTER 3    Exponential and Logarithmic Functions

16.    Use a calculator to evaluate $\log_6 21.3$ to four decimal places.

17.    Solve for x to two decimal places (using a calculator):
       $900 = 700(1.08)^x$

18.    If \$2,000 is invested at 9% compounded annually, how long will it
       take for it to grow to \$4,000, assuming no withdrawals are made?
       Compute answer to the next higher year if not exact. $[A = P(1 + r)^t]$

19.    A country has a population growth rate of 2.3% compounded
       continuously.  At this rate, how long will it take for the
       population of the country to double?

20.    A carbon-14 dating test is performed on a fossil bone, and analysis
       finds that 19.5% of the original amount of $^{14}C$ is still present
       in the bone.  Estimate the age of the fossil bone.
       (Recall that $^{14}C$ decays according to the equation $A = A_0 e^{-0.000124t}$.)

Key Sheet - CHAPTER 3

[1]  $7^{6x}$

[2]  $\dfrac{3^{6x^2}}{2^{4xy}}$

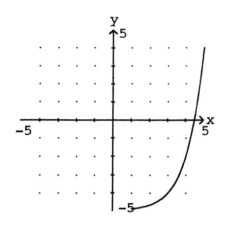

[3]

[4]  x = 3

[5]  9,418 bacteria

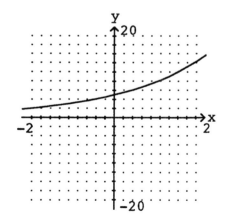

[6]

Key Sheet - CHAPTER 3

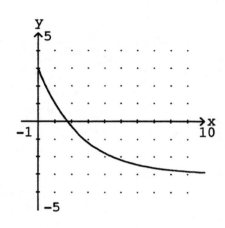

[7]
_____

[8]  $e^{6x} + 6 + 9e^{-2x}$

[9]  $2,479.72

[10]  $27 = 9^{3/2}$

[11]  $\log_4 16 = 2$

[12]  3

[13]  x = 2

[14]  x = 4

[15]  (A) log 0.35 = -0.4559    (B) ln 47 = 3.8501

[16]  1.7071

[17]  x = 3.27

[18]  9 years

[19]  t = 30.1 years

[20]  t ≈ 13,184 years

Essentials of College Mathematics, Third Edition
Raymond A. Barnett and Michael R. Ziegler

Form A-C

CHAPTER 3     Exponential and Logarithmic Functions

1.   Simplify: $\dfrac{2^{5x+7}}{2^{7-2x}}$

2.   Simplify: $\left(\dfrac{3^{2x}}{2^{3y}}\right)^{3x}$

3.   Graph $y = 3^{x-2} - 4$ over the interval $[0, 4]$.

4.   Solve for x: $2^{4x} = 8^{x+5}$

5.   A particular bacterium is found to have a doubling time of 40 minutes.  If a laboratory culture begins with a population of 900 of this bacteria and there is no change in the growth rate, how many bacteria will be present in 95 minutes?

6.   Graph $y = 4e^{-x/4}$, $-2 \le x \le 2$, using a calculator.  Choose horizontal and vertical scales as follows:

     Horizontal scale: 1 unit = 5 squares;
     Vertical scale: 1 unit = 1/2 square

7.   Graph $y = 9e^{-0.4x} - 4$ over $[0, 10]$.

8.   Simplify: $e^{4x}(e^x - e^{-2x}) + (e^x + 2e^{-x})^2$

9.   If you invest \$2,000 in an account paying 8.35% compounded continuously, how much money will be in the account after 18 years?

10.  Rewrite in equivalent exponential form: $\log_4 2 = \frac{1}{2}$

11.  Rewrite in equivalent logarithmic form: $6^4 = 1296$

12.  Evaluate: $\log_7 7^5$

13.  Solve for x without using a calculator or table:
     $\log_b x - \log_b 9 = \log_b 7 - \log_b(x - 2)$

14.  Solve for x:  $\log_{10} x + \log_{10}(x - 8) = \log_{10} 9$

15.  Use a calculator to evaluate: (A) log 0.29    (B) ln 327

CHAPTER 3    Exponential and Logarithmic Functions

16.    Use a calculator to evaluate $\log_8 36.8$ to four decimal places.

17.    Solve for x to two decimal places (using a calculator):
       $300 = 100(1.07)^x$

18.    If \$4,000 is invested at 11% compounded annually, how long will it
       take for it to grow to \$6,000, assuming no withdrawals are made?
       Compute answer to the next higher year if not exact. $[A = P(1 + r)^t]$

19.    A country has a population growth rate of 3.6% compounded
       continuously. At this rate, how long will it take for the
       population of the country to double?

20.    A carbon-14 dating test is performed on a fossil bone, and analysis
       finds that 3.5% of the original amount of $^{14}C$ is still present
       in the bone. Estimate the age of the fossil bone.
       (Recall that $^{14}C$ decays according to the equation $A = A_0 e^{-0.000124t}$.)

Key Sheet - CHAPTER 3

[1]  $2^{7x}$

[2]  $\dfrac{3^{6x^2}}{2^{9xy}}$

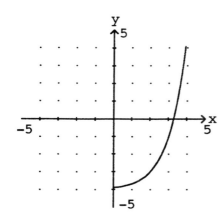

[3]

[4]  x = 15

[5]  4,669 bacteria

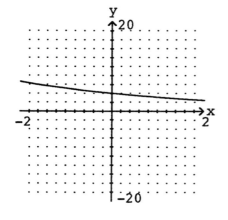

[6]

Key Sheet - CHAPTER 3

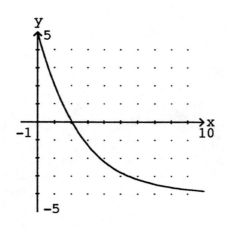

[7]

[8] $e^{5x} + 4 + 4e^{-2x}$

[9] $8,990.31

[10] $2 = 4^{1/2}$

[11] $\log_6 1296 = 4$

[12] 5

[13] $x = 9$

[14] $x = 9$

[15] (A) $\log 0.29 = -0.5376$    (B) $\ln 327 = 5.7900$

[16] 1.7339

[17] $x = 16.24$

[18] 4 years

[19] $t = 19.3$ years

[20] $t \approx 27,036$ years

# DellenTest MAC 2.0

Copyright © 1995 by Prentice-Hall, Inc.

Essentials of College Mathematics, Third Edition
Raymond A. Barnett and Michael R. Ziegler

CHAPTER 4    Mathematics of Finance

1.  Find the amount due on a loan of $8,900 at 14.5% simple interest at the end of 4.0 years.

2.  If you pay $5,250 for a simple interest note that will be worth $6,000 in 21 months, what annual simple interest rate will you earn? (Compute the answer to one decimal place.)

3.  If an investor buys a 26 week T-bill with a maturity value of $5,000 for $4,766, what annual interest rate will the investor earn? (Express your answer as a percentage, and correct to one decimal place.)

4.  An investor purchased 500 shares of a stock at $20 per share. The commission she paid to buy the stock was $65 plus 0.3% of the principal amount. Six months later she sold the stock for $21.50 per share. If she paid the same rate of commission to sell the stock, what annual rate of interest did she earn on her initial investment (including purchase price plus commission)? Express your answer as a percentage, correct to one decimal place.

5.  What amount will be in an account after 5.0 years if $4,000 is invested at 9% compounded semiannually?

6.  How much should you invest now at 8% compounded semiannually to have $8,000 to buy a car in 2.0 years?

7.  A savings and loan pays 12% compounded quarterly. What is the effective rate? (Compute the answer to two decimal places.)

8.  How many quarters will it take until an account will have $6,000 if $500 is invested now at 9% compounded quarterly?

9.  What is the future value of an ordinary annuity at the end of 5 years if $100 is deposited each quarter into an account earning 9% compounded quarterly?

10. An ordinary annuity has a value of $874.92 at the end of 4 years when $200 is deposited every year into an account earning 6% compounded annually. How much interest has been earned?

11. You deposit $100 each month into a savings account that pays 8% compounded monthly. How much interest will you have earned after 10 years?

12. A company establishes a sinking fund to replace equipment at an estimated cost of $150,000 in 7 years. How much should be invested each year into an account paying 12% compounded annually in order to have $150,000 in 7 years?

CHAPTER 4    Mathematics of Finance

13. You can afford annual deposits of only $150 into an account
    that pays 15% compounded annually.  How many years will it
    be until you have $9,500 to buy a car?  (Round up to the next
    higher year if not an integer.)

14. A couple decides on the following savings plan for their child's
    college education.  When the child is 6 months old, and every 6
    months thereafter, they will deposit $360 into a savings account
    paying 10% interest compounded semiannually.  After the child's
    tenth birthday, having made 20 such payments, they will stop making
    deposits and let the accumulated money earn interest, at the same
    rate, for 8 more years, until the child is 18 years old and ready
    for college.  How much money (to the nearest dollar) will be in the
    account when the child is ready for college?

15. What is the present value of an ordinary annuity that pays $400 per
    quarter for 3 years if money is worth 12% compounded quarterly?

16. You have decided to buy a new stereo system for $2,000 and agreed
    to pay in 30 equal monthly payments at 1.75% interest per month
    on the unpaid balance.  How much are your payments?

17. You have purchased a new house and have a mortgage for $65,000 at
    9%.  The loan is amortized over 30 years in equal monthly payments
    of $523.00.  Find the total amount paid in interest when the mortgage
    is paid off.

18. A bank makes a home mortgage loan of $160,000 at 13% amortized
    in equal monthly payments over 30 years.  What is the total amount
    paid in interest when the mortgage is paid off (round to the nearest
    dollar)?

19. A $8,000 debt is to be amortized in 15 equal monthly payments of
    $565.89 at 0.75% interest per month on the unpaid balance.  What is
    the unpaid balance after the second payment?

20. You have agreed to pay off a $8,000 loan in 30 monthly payments of
    $321.43 per month.  The interest rate of the loan is 1.25% per month
    on the unpaid balance.  What is the unpaid balance after 6 monthly
    payments have been made?

21. A couple wishes to borrow $65,000 in order to buy a house.  They can
    pay a maximum of $825 per month.  If the loan is at 8.5% compounded
    monthly, how many months will it take to pay off the loan?  (Round
    answer to next higher month if not an integer.)

22. A home was purchased 12 years ago for $60,000.  The home was financed
    by paying 20% down payment and signing a 30 year mortgage at 8.5%
    compounded monthly on the unpaid balance.  The market value is now
    $100,000.  The owner wishes to sell the house.  How much equity (to
    the nearest dollar) does the owner have in the house after making 144
    monthly payments?

Key Sheet - CHAPTER 4

[1]   $14,062.00

[2]   8.2%

[3]   9.8%

[4]   11.1%

[5]   $6,211.88

[6]   $6,838.43

[7]   12.55%

[8]   112 quarters

[9]   $2,491.15

[10]  $74.92

[11]  $6,294.60

[12]  $14,867.66

[13]  17 years

[14]  $25,984

[15]  $3,981.60

[16]  $86.26

[17]  $123,280.00

[18]  $477,171

[19]  $6,984.43

[20]  $6,629.21

[21]  116 months

[22]  $59,238

## DellenTest MAC 2.0
Copyright © 1995 by Prentice-Hall, Inc.

Essentials of College Mathematics, Third Edition
Raymond A. Barnett and Michael R. Ziegler

Form A-B

Page 1

### CHAPTER 4    Mathematics of Finance

1. Find the amount due on a loan of $9,100 at 17.5% simple interest at the end of 3.0 years.

2. If you pay $5,250 for a simple interest note that will be worth $7,000 in 24 months, what annual simple interest rate will you earn? (Compute the answer to one decimal place.)

3. If an investor buys a 26 week T-bill with a maturity value of $30,000 for $28,355, what annual interest rate will the investor earn? (Express your answer as a percentage, and correct to one decimal place.)

4. An investor purchased 500 shares of a stock at $18 per share. The commission she paid to buy the stock was $65 plus 0.3% of the principal amount. Six months later she sold the stock for $19.50 per share. If she paid the same rate of commission to sell the stock, what annual rate of interest did she earn on her initial investment (including purchase price plus commission)? Express your answer as a percentage, correct to one decimal place.

5. What amount will be in an account after 3.0 years if $5,000 is invested at 12% compounded quarterly?

6. How much should you invest now at 8% compounded quarterly to have $8,500 to buy a car in 2.0 years?

7. A bank pays 6% compounded monthly. What is the effective rate? (Compute the answer to two decimal places.)

8. How many months will it take until an account will have $4,000 if $2,500 is invested now at 9% compounded monthly?

9. What is the future value of an ordinary annuity at the end of 5 years if $450 is deposited each month into an account earning 6% compounded monthly?

10. An ordinary annuity has a value of $12,049.26 at the end of 6 years when $350 is deposited every quarter into an account earning 12% compounded quarterly. How much interest has been earned?

11. You deposit $130 each month into a savings account that pays 10% compounded monthly. How much interest will you have earned after 5 years?

12. A company establishes a sinking fund to replace equipment at an estimated cost of $100,000 in 9 years. How much should be invested each month into an account paying 9% compounded monthly in order to have $100,000 in 9 years?

CHAPTER 4    Mathematics of Finance

13. You can afford monthly deposits of only $50 into an account that pays 12% compounded monthly. How many months will it be until you have $7,500 to buy a car? (Round up to the next higher month if not an integer.)

14. A couple decides on the following savings plan for their child's college education. When the child is 6 months old, and every 6 months thereafter, they will deposit $330 into a savings account paying 9% interest compounded semiannually. After the child's tenth birthday, having made 20 such payments, they will stop making deposits and let the accumulated money earn interest, at the same rate, for 8 more years, until the child is 18 years old and ready for college. How much money (to the nearest dollar) will be in the account when the child is ready for college?

15. What is the present value of an ordinary annuity that pays $200 per month for 6 years if money is worth 6% compounded monthly?

16. You have decided to buy a new micro-computer for $3,000 and agreed to pay in 36 equal monthly payments at 1.75% interest per month on the unpaid balance. How much are your payments?

17. You have purchased a new house and have a mortgage for $60,000 at 15%. The loan is amortized over 20 years in equal monthly payments of $790.07. Find the total amount paid in interest when the mortgage is paid off.

18. A bank makes a home mortgage loan of $170,000 at 11.5% amortized in equal monthly payments over 30 years. What is the total amount paid in interest when the mortgage is paid off (round to the nearest dollar)?

19. A $8,000 debt is to be amortized in 12 equal monthly payments of $722.07 at 1.25% interest per month on the unpaid balance. What is the unpaid balance after the second payment?

20. You have agreed to pay off a $6,000 loan in 30 monthly payments of $232.49 per month. The interest rate of the loan is 1.00% per month on the unpaid balance. What is the unpaid balance after 12 monthly payments have been made?

21. A couple wishes to borrow $55,000 in order to buy a house. They can pay a maximum of $900 per month. If the loan is at 8.0% compounded monthly, how many months will it take to pay off the loan? (Round answer to next higher month if not an integer.)

22. A home was purchased 16 years ago for $60,000. The home was financed by paying 20% down payment and signing a 30 year mortgage at 8.0% compounded monthly on the unpaid balance. The market value is now $100,000. The owner wishes to sell the house. How much equity (to the nearest dollar) does the owner have in the house after making 192 monthly payments?

## Key Sheet - CHAPTER 4

[1]  $13,877.50

[2]  16.7%

[3]  11.6%

[4]  12.4%

[5]  $7,128.80

[6]  $7,254.67

[7]  6.17%

[8]  63 months

[9]  $31,396.51

[10] $3,649.26

[11] $2,266.82

[12] $604.29

[13] 93 months

[14] $20,937

[15] $12,067.90

[16] $113.03

[17] $129,616.80

[18] $436,058

[19] $6,748.08

[20] $3,812.41

[21] 79 months

[22] $64,471

# DellenTest MAC 2.0
Copyright © 1995 by Prentice-Hall, Inc.

Essentials of College Mathematics, Third Edition
Raymond A. Barnett and Michael R. Ziegler

Form A-C
Page 1

## CHAPTER 4    Mathematics of Finance

1.  Find the amount due on a loan of $9,300 at 17.5% simple interest at the end of 2.5 years.

2.  If you pay $5,250 for a simple interest note that will be worth $6,500 in 24 months, what annual simple interest rate will you earn? (Compute the answer to one decimal place.)

3.  If an investor buys a 39 week T-bill with a maturity value of $25,000 for $23,552, what annual interest rate will the investor earn? (Express your answer as a percentage, and correct to one decimal place.)

4.  An investor purchased 500 shares of a stock at $15 per share. The commission she paid to buy the stock was $65 plus 0.3% of the principal amount. Six months later she sold the stock for $16.50 per share. If she paid the same rate of commission to sell the stock, what annual rate of interest did she earn on her initial investment (including purchase price plus commission)? Express your answer as a percentage, correct to one decimal place.

5.  What amount will be in an account after 1.5 years if $5,000 is invested at 6% compounded monthly?

6.  How much should you invest now at 12% compounded semiannually to have $8,500 to buy a car in 2.0 years?

7.  An investment company pays 6% compounded semiannually. What is the effective rate? (Compute the answer to two decimal places.)

8.  How many half years will it take until an account will have $5,000 if $1,000 is invested now at 9% compounded semiannually?

9.  What is the future value of an ordinary annuity at the end of 7 years if $150 is deposited each 6 months into an account earning 6% compounded semiannually?

10. An ordinary annuity has a value of $22,829.94 at the end of 4 years when $350 is deposited every month into an account earning 15% compounded monthly. How much interest has been earned?

11. You deposit $150 each month into a savings account that pays 9% compounded monthly. How much interest will you have earned after 10 years?

12. A company establishes a sinking fund to replace equipment at an estimated cost of $200,000 in 9 years. How much should be invested each quarter into an account paying 12% compounded quarterly in order to have $200,000 in 9 years?

CHAPTER 4     Mathematics of Finance

13. You can afford quarterly deposits of only $150 into an account that pays 6% compounded quarterly. How many quarters will it be until you have $8,500 to buy a car? (Round up to the next higher quarter if not an integer.)

14. A couple decides on the following savings plan for their child's college education. When the child is 6 months old, and every 6 months thereafter, they will deposit $310 into a savings account paying 8% interest compounded semiannually. After the child's tenth birthday, having made 20 such payments, they will stop making deposits and let the accumulated money earn interest, at the same rate, for 8 more years, until the child is 18 years old and ready for college. How much money (to the nearest dollar) will be in the account when the child is ready for college?

15. What is the present value of an ordinary annuity that pays $250 per year for 4 years if money is worth 12% compounded annually?

16. You have decided to buy a new stereo system for $2,000 and agreed to pay in 30 equal monthly payments at 2.00% interest per month on the unpaid balance. How much are your payments?

17. You have purchased a new house and have a mortgage for $60,000 at 12%. The loan is amortized over 30 years in equal monthly payments of $617.17. Find the total amount paid in interest when the mortgage is paid off.

18. A bank makes a home mortgage loan of $230,000 at 10% amortized in equal monthly payments over 30 years. What is the total amount paid in interest when the mortgage is paid off (round to the nearest dollar)?

19. A $7,000 debt is to be amortized in 18 equal monthly payments of $426.87 at 1.00% interest per month on the unpaid balance. What is the unpaid balance after the second payment?

20. You have agreed to pay off an $8,000 loan in 30 monthly payments of $298.79 per month. The interest rate of the loan is 0.75% per month on the unpaid balance. What is the unpaid balance after 12 monthly payments have been made?

21. A couple wishes to borrow $65,000 in order to buy a house. They can pay a maximum of $900 per month. If the loan is at 9.0% compounded monthly, how many months will it take to pay off the loan? (Round answer to next higher month if not an integer.)

22. A home was purchased 14 years ago for $65,000. The home was financed by paying 20% down payment and signing a 25 year mortgage at 9.0% compounded monthly on the unpaid balance. The market value is now $100,000. The owner wishes to sell the house. How much equity (to the nearest dollar) does the owner have in the house after making 168 monthly payments?

Key Sheet - CHAPTER 4

[1]  $13,368.75
_____

[2]  11.9%
_____

[3]  8.2%
_____

[4]  15.1%
_____

[5]  $5,469.64
_____

[6]  $6,732.80
_____

[7]  6.09%
_____

[8]  37 half years
_____

[9]  $2,562.95
_____

[10] $6,029.94
_____

[11] $11,027.14
_____

[12] $3,160.76
_____

[13] 42 quarters
_____

[14] $17,290
_____

[15] $759.34
_____

[16] $89.30
_____

[17] $162,181.20
_____

[18] $496,629
_____

[19] $6,282.69
_____

[20] $5,013.37
_____

[21] 105 months
_____

[22] $63,516
_____

Essentials of College Mathematics, Third Edition
Raymond A. Barnett and Michael R. Ziegler

CHAPTER 5    Systems of Linear Equations; Matrices

1.    Solve graphically: $3x + 2y = 5$
$2x - 3y = 12$

2.    Solve by elimination using addition: $4x - 2y = 8$
$5x + 2y = 19$

3.    Solve by elimination using addition: $4x - 10y = 4$
$6x - 15y = -6$

4.    A company that manufactures laser printers for computers has monthly fixed costs of $150,500 and variable costs of $650 per unit produced.  The company sells the printers for $1,350 per unit. How many printers must be sold each month for the company to break even?

5.    Only one of the following augmented matrices of a linear system is in a reduced form.  Indicate by letter which one.

(A) $\begin{bmatrix} 1 & 0 & | & 3 \\ 0 & 0 & | & 0 \\ 0 & 1 & | & -1 \end{bmatrix}$   (B) $\begin{bmatrix} 0 & 1 & | & 5 \\ 1 & 0 & | & -5 \end{bmatrix}$   (C) $\begin{bmatrix} 1 & 0 & -5 & | & 4 \\ 0 & 0 & 1 & | & -3 \end{bmatrix}$   (D) $\begin{bmatrix} 1 & -5 & 0 & | & -5 \\ 0 & 0 & 1 & | & 2 \\ 0 & 0 & 0 & | & 0 \end{bmatrix}$

6.    The reduced forms for three systems of equations are given below. Indicate by letter which system has no solution.

(A) $\begin{bmatrix} 1 & 0 & | & 4 \\ 0 & 1 & | & 1 \\ 0 & 0 & | & 0 \end{bmatrix}$   (B) $\begin{bmatrix} 1 & 0 & -2 & | & -1 \\ 0 & 1 & -4 & | & 3 \\ 0 & 0 & 0 & | & 1 \end{bmatrix}$   (C) $\begin{bmatrix} 1 & 3 & 0 & | & 4 \\ 0 & 0 & 1 & | & 2 \\ 0 & 0 & 0 & | & 0 \end{bmatrix}$

7.    Solve the linear system corresponding to the following augmented matrix:

$\begin{bmatrix} 1 & 0 & -3 & | & 3 \\ 0 & 1 & -3 & | & -4 \\ 0 & 0 & 0 & | & 0 \end{bmatrix}$

8.    Solve by augmented matrix methods using Gauss-Jordan elimination:

$x_1 - 2x_2 - 3x_3 = -6$
$x_2 - 3x_3 = -8$
$x_1 + x_3 = -2$

---

CHAPTER 5    Systems of Linear Equations; Matrices

---

9.  Solve by augmented matrix methods using Gauss-Jordan elimination:

$$4x_1 + 2x_2 = -18$$
$$2x_1 - 4x_2 = 6$$
$$2x_1 + x_2 = -9$$

10. Solve by augmented matrix methods using Gauss-Jordan elimination:

$$x_1 + x_2 + 5x_3 - x_4 = 8$$
$$x_1 - x_2 + 5x_3 + x_4 = 6$$

11. A performance center has 2,000 seats.  Tickets for an event are $5
    and $8 per seat.  Assuming that all tickets are sold and bring in a
    total of $11,500, how many of each type of ticket were sold?  Set up
    a system of equations and solve by augmented matrix methods using
    Gauss-Jordan elimination.

12. If $5,000 is to be invested, part at 14% and the rest at 7%, how
    much should be invested at each rate so that the total annual return
    will be the same as $5,000 invested at 9%?  Set up a system of
    linear equations, letting $x_1$ be the amount invested at 14% and
    $x_2$ be the amount invested at 7%.  DO NOT SOLVE THE SYSTEM.

13. Unit labor and material costs for manufacturing each of three types of
    products M, N, and P are given in the table:

    |           | Product |      |      |
    |-----------|---------|------|------|
    |           | M       | N    | P    |
    | Labor     | $60     | $30  | $30  |
    | Materials | $70     | $10  | $50  |

    The weekly allocation for labor is $60,000 and for materials is
    $90,000.  There are to be 2 times as many units of product M
    manufactured as units of product P.  How many of each type of product
    should be manufactured each week to use exactly each of the weekly
    allocations?  Set up a system of linear equations, letting $x_1$, $x_2$,
    and $x_3$ be the number of units of products M, N, and P, respectively,
    manufactured in one week.  DO NOT SOLVE THE SYSTEM.

CHAPTER 5   Systems of Linear Equations; Matrices

14.  In producing three types of bricks: face bricks, common bricks, and
     refractory bricks, a factory incurs labor, material, and utility
     costs.  To produce one pallet of face bricks, the labor, material,
     and utility costs are $40, $80, and $35, respectively.  To produce
     one pallet of common bricks, the labor, material, and utility costs
     are $40, $65, and $30, respectively, while the corresponding
     costs for refractory bricks are $65, $105, and $45.  In a certain
     month the company has allocated $11,500 for labor costs, $14,000 for
     material costs and $5,000 for utility costs.  How many pallets of each
     type of brick should be produced in that month to exactly utilize
     these allocations?  Set up a system of linear equations, letting x, y,
     and z be the number of pallets of face, common, and refractory bricks,
     respectively, that must be produced in that month.  DO NOT SOLVE THE
     SYSTEM.

15.  A paper company produces high, medium, and low grade paper.  The
     number of tons of each grade that is produced from one ton of pulp
     depends on the source of that pulp.  The following table lists three
     sources and the amount of each grade of paper that can be made from
     one ton of pulp from each source.

|                | (Number of Tons) | | |
|                | High Grade | Medium Grade | Low Grade |
|----------------|------------|--------------|-----------|
| Brazilian Pulp | 0.5        | 0.2          | 0.3       |
| Domestic Pulp  | 0.4        | 0.2          | 0.4       |
| Recycled Pulp  | 0.2        | 0.3          | 0.5       |

The paper company has orders for 13 tons of high grade, 15 tons of
medium grade, and 14 tons of low grade paper.  How many tons of
each type of pulp should be used to fill these orders exactly?  Set
up a system of linear equations, letting x, y, z be the number of
tons of Brazilian pulp, domestic pulp, and recycled pulp,
respectively, needed to fill the orders.  DO NOT SOLVE THE SYSTEM.

16.  A hospital dietician wants to insure that a certain meal consisting
     of rice, broccoli, and fish contains exactly 41,400 units of vitamin
     A, 1,360 units of vitamin E, and 4,640 units of vitamin C.  One ounce
     of rice contains 600 units of vitamin A, 20 units of vitamin E, and
     160 units of vitamin C.  One ounce of broccoli contains 1200 units of
     vitamin A, 60 units of vitamin E, and 480 units of vitamin C.  And
     one ounce of fish contains 5,400 units of vitamin A, 160 units of
     vitamin E, and 240 units of vitamin C.  How many ounces of each food
     should this meal include?  Set up a system of linear equations and
     solve using Gauss-Jordan elimination.

CHAPTER 5    Systems of Linear Equations; Matrices

17. A trucking firm wants to purchase 12 trucks that will provide exactly 33 tons of additional shipping capacity. A model A truck holds 2 tons, a model B truck holds 3 tons, and a model C truck holds 6 tons. How many trucks of each model should the company purchase to provide the additional shipping capacity? Set up a system of linear equations and solve using Gauss-Jordan elimination.

18. Find:
$$-2\begin{bmatrix} -1 & 0 & 1 \\ 3 & 1 & 0 \\ 0 & 1 & -1 \end{bmatrix} + \begin{bmatrix} 2 & 0 & 0 \\ -4 & 0 & 1 \\ 2 & -1 & -1 \end{bmatrix}$$

19. Given $A = \begin{bmatrix} 3 \\ 1 \\ -1 \end{bmatrix}$ and $B = [1 \ -4 \ 0]$, find AB.

20. Given $A = \begin{bmatrix} 1 & 4 & 0 \\ 2 & -1 & 0 \end{bmatrix}$ and $B = \begin{bmatrix} 1 & -3 \\ 0 & 1 \\ 1 & -1 \end{bmatrix}$, find AB.

21. A retail company offers, through two different stores in a city, three models, A, B, and C, of a particular brand of camping stove. The inventory of each model on hand in each store is summarized in matrix M. Wholesale (W) and retail (R) prices of each model are summarized in matrix N. Find the product MN and label its columns and rows appropriately. What is the wholesale value of the inventory in Store 1?

$$M = \begin{matrix} & A & B & C \\ & \begin{bmatrix} 2 & 0 & 1 \\ 4 & 2 & 0 \end{bmatrix} \end{matrix} \begin{matrix} \text{Store 1} \\ \text{Store 2} \end{matrix} \qquad N = \begin{matrix} W & R \\ \begin{bmatrix} \$100 & \$150 \\ \$40 & \$50 \\ \$60 & \$75 \end{bmatrix} \end{matrix} \begin{matrix} A \\ B \\ C \end{matrix}$$

CHAPTER 5    Systems of Linear Equations; Matrices

22.  A supermarket chain sells oranges, apples, peaches, and bananas in three stores located throughout a large metropolitan area.  The average number of pounds sold per day in each store is summarized in matrix M.  "In season" and "out of season" prices, per pound, of each fruit are given in matrix N.  What is the total, for the three stores, of "in season" daily revenue for the four fruits? The "out of season" peach sales represent what percentage of the daily total "out of season" revenues for Store 3?

$$M = \begin{bmatrix} 75 & 75 & 75 & 40 \\ 85 & 70 & 90 & 50 \\ 65 & 85 & 45 & 90 \end{bmatrix} \begin{matrix} \text{Store 1} \\ \text{Store 2} \\ \text{Store 3} \end{matrix}$$

Fruit: O  A  P  B

$$N = \begin{bmatrix} \$3.50 & \$8.00 \\ \$5.50 & \$9.50 \\ \$5.00 & \$4.50 \\ \$0.40 & \$0.60 \end{bmatrix} \begin{matrix} O \\ A \\ P \\ B \end{matrix}$$

"In Season"   "Out of Season"

23.  Use Gauss-Jordan elimination to find the inverse of $\begin{bmatrix} 1 & 1 \\ 4 & 5 \end{bmatrix}$.

24.  Use Gauss-Jordan elimination, without introducing fractions, to find the inverse of $\begin{bmatrix} 3 & -4 & 2 \\ 0 & 1 & 0 \\ 1 & 0 & 1 \end{bmatrix}$.

25.  The following message was encoded with the matrix $A = \begin{bmatrix} 1 & 1 \\ 4 & 5 \end{bmatrix}$ Decode this message.

28 120 32 155 30 125 24 108 38 175 30 123 21 104 36 153
46 211 27 123 39 176

26.  Use $\begin{bmatrix} -9 & 8 \\ 1 & -1 \end{bmatrix}^{-1} = \begin{bmatrix} -1 & -8 \\ -1 & -9 \end{bmatrix}$ to solve: $\begin{aligned} -9x_1 + 8x_2 &= 3 \\ x_1 - x_2 &= -3 \end{aligned}$

27.  Use $\begin{bmatrix} 1 & -2 & 2 \\ 1 & 1 & 0 \\ 1 & 0 & 1 \end{bmatrix}^{-1} = \begin{bmatrix} 1 & 2 & -2 \\ -1 & -1 & 2 \\ -1 & -2 & 3 \end{bmatrix}$ to solve: $\begin{aligned} x_1 - 2x_2 + 2x_3 &= -3 \\ x_1 + x_2 &= 0 \\ x_1 + x_3 &= 1 \end{aligned}$

CHAPTER 5    Systems of Linear Equations; Matrices

28.  A chain of amusement parks pays experienced workers $275 per week
     and inexperienced workers $250 per week.  The total number of workers
     and the total weekly wages at three different parks are given in the
     table.  How many experienced workers does each park employ?  Set up
     a system of linear equations and solve using matrix inverse methods.

|                    | Park 1 | Park 2 | Park 3 |
|--------------------|--------|--------|--------|
| Number of workers  | 150    | 125    | 200    |
| Total weekly wages | 38,125 | 33,125 | 52,500 |

## Key Sheet – CHAPTER 5

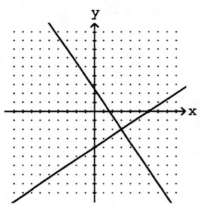

[1]   $x = 3$, $y = -2$

[2]   $x = 3$, $y = 2$

[3]   no solution

[4]   215 printers per month

[5]   (D)

[6]   (B)

$x_1 = 3t + 3$
$x_2 = 3t - 4$
$x_3 = t$
[7]   $t$ = any real number

$x_1 = -4$
$x_2 = -2$
$x_3 = 2$
[8]

$x_1 = -3$
$x_2 = -3$
[9]

$x_1 = -5s + 7$
$x_2 = t + 1$
$x_3 = s$
$x_4 = t$
[10]  $s$ and $t$ any real numbers

## Key Sheet - CHAPTER 5

[11] 1,500 $5 seats
500 $8 seats

[12]
$$x_1 + x_2 = 5,000$$
$$0.14x_1 + 0.07x_2 = 450$$

[13]
$$60x_1 + 30x_2 + 30x_3 = 60,000$$
$$70x_1 + 10x_2 + 50x_3 = 90,000$$
$$x_1 - 2x_3 = 0$$

[14]
$$40x + 40y + 65z = 11,500$$
$$80x + 65y + 105z = 14,000$$
$$35x + 30y + 45z = 5,000$$

[15]
$$0.5x + 0.4y + 0.2z = 13$$
$$0.2x + 0.2y + 0.3z = 15$$
$$0.3x + 0.4y + 0.5z = 14$$

[16] 5 ounces rice, 5 ounces broccoli, 6 ounces fish

[17] 3 model A, 9 model B, and 0 model C trucks; or
6 model A, 5 model B, and 1 model C trucks; or
9 model A, 1 model B, and 2 model C trucks

[18]
$$\begin{bmatrix} 4 & 3 & -2 \\ -10 & -2 & 1 \\ 2 & -3 & 1 \end{bmatrix}$$

[19]
$$\begin{bmatrix} 3 & -12 & 0 \\ 1 & -4 & 0 \\ -1 & 4 & 0 \end{bmatrix}$$

[20]
$$\begin{bmatrix} 1 & 3 \\ 2 & -7 \end{bmatrix}$$

[21]
$$\begin{matrix} & W & R \\ \begin{bmatrix} \$260 & \$375 \\ \$480 & \$700 \end{bmatrix} & \text{Store 1} & \$260 \\ & \text{Store 2} & \end{matrix}$$

[22] $3174.5;   12.78%

[23]
$$\begin{bmatrix} 5 & -1 \\ -4 & 1 \end{bmatrix}$$

[24]
$$\begin{bmatrix} 1 & 4 & -2 \\ 0 & 1 & 0 \\ -1 & -4 & 3 \end{bmatrix}$$

[25] THE YELLOW CAT IS LOST

## Key Sheet – CHAPTER 5

[26]
$$x_1 = 21$$
$$x_2 = 24$$

[27]
$$x_1 = -5$$
$$x_2 = 5$$
$$x_3 = 6$$

[28]
**Park 1: 25 experienced workers**
**Park 2: 75 experienced workers**
**Park 3: 100 experienced workers**

Essentials of College Mathematics, Third Edition
Raymond A. Barnett and Michael R. Ziegler

CHAPTER 5    Systems of Linear Equations; Matrices

1.    Solve graphically: $2x + y = 11$
$2x - y = 5$

2.    Solve by elimination using addition: $3x - 3y = 18$

$4x + 4y = -8$

3.    Solve by elimination using addition: $6x - 8y = 8$

$9x - 12y = -12$

4.    A company that manufactures laser printers for computers has monthly fixed costs of $123,000 and variable costs of $750 per unit produced.  The company sells the printers for $1,350 per unit. How many printers must be sold each month for the company to break even?

5.    Only one of the following augmented matrices of a linear system is in a reduced form.  Indicate by letter which one.

(A) $\begin{bmatrix} 1 & 5 & 0 & | & 4 \\ 0 & 0 & 1 & | & 4 \\ 0 & 0 & 0 & | & 0 \end{bmatrix}$    (B) $\begin{bmatrix} 1 & 0 & | & 4 \\ 0 & 0 & | & 0 \\ 0 & 1 & | & -5 \end{bmatrix}$    (C) $\begin{bmatrix} 0 & 1 & | & 1 \\ 1 & 0 & | & 5 \end{bmatrix}$    (D) $\begin{bmatrix} 1 & 0 & 2 & | & -5 \\ 0 & 0 & 1 & | & -5 \end{bmatrix}$

6.    The reduced forms for three systems of equations are given below. Indicate by letter which system has infinitely many solutions.

(A) $\begin{bmatrix} 1 & 0 & | & -2 \\ 0 & 1 & | & -5 \\ 0 & 0 & | & 0 \end{bmatrix}$    (B) $\begin{bmatrix} 1 & -4 & 0 & | & -4 \\ 0 & 0 & 1 & | & -3 \\ 0 & 0 & 0 & | & 0 \end{bmatrix}$    (C) $\begin{bmatrix} 1 & 0 & 3 & | & -5 \\ 0 & 1 & 3 & | & 3 \\ 0 & 0 & 0 & | & 1 \end{bmatrix}$

7.    Solve the linear system corresponding to the following augmented matrix:

$\begin{bmatrix} 1 & 0 & 1 & | & -5 \\ 0 & 1 & -5 & | & 3 \\ 0 & 0 & 1 & | & 1 \end{bmatrix}$

8.    Solve by augmented matrix methods using Gauss-Jordan elimination:

$x_1 - 3x_2 - 3x_3 = -1$

$x_2 - 3x_3 = -9$

$x_1 \qquad + x_3 = -2$

CHAPTER 5    Systems of Linear Equations; Matrices

9.  Solve by augmented matrix methods using Gauss-Jordan elimination:

$$4x_1 + 4x_2 = 4$$
$$4x_1 - 4x_2 = -20$$
$$2x_1 + 2x_2 = 2$$

10. Solve by augmented matrix methods using Gauss-Jordan elimination:

$$x_1 + x_2 + 5x_3 - 2x_4 = 2$$
$$x_1 - x_2 + 5x_3 + 2x_4 = 4$$

11. A performance center has 2,400 seats.  Tickets for an event are $5
    and $8 per seat.  Assuming that all tickets are sold and bring in a
    total of $14,400, how many of each type of ticket were sold?  Set up
    a system of equations and solve by augmented matrix methods using
    Gauss-Jordan elimination.

12. If $9,000 is to be invested, part at 14% and the rest at 7%, how
    much should be invested at each rate so that the total annual return
    will be the same as $9,000 invested at 9%?  Set up a system of
    linear equations, letting $x_1$ be the amount invested at 14% and
    $x_2$ be the amount invested at 7%.  DO NOT SOLVE THE SYSTEM.

13. Unit labor and material costs for manufacturing each of three types of
    products M, N, and P are given in the table:

    |           | Product |      |      |
    |-----------|---------|------|------|
    |           | M       | N    | P    |
    | Labor     | $60     | $40  | $20  |
    | Materials | $70     | $20  | $40  |

    The weekly allocation for labor is $60,000 and for materials is
    $90,000.  There are to be 3 times as many units of product M
    manufactured as units of product P.  How many of each type of product
    should be manufactured each week to use exactly each of the weekly
    allocations?  Set up a system of linear equations, letting $x_1$, $x_2$,
    and $x_3$ be the number of units of products M, N, and P, respectively,
    manufactured in one week.  DO NOT SOLVE THE SYSTEM.

CHAPTER 5    Systems of Linear Equations; Matrices

14. In producing three types of bricks: face bricks, common bricks, and refractory bricks, a factory incurs labor, material, and utility costs. To produce one pallet of face bricks, the labor, material, and utility costs are $60, $70, and $35, respectively. To produce one pallet of common bricks, the labor, material, and utility costs are $60, $55, and $30, respectively, while the corresponding costs for refractory bricks are $85, $95, and $45. In a certain month the company has allocated $11,500 for labor costs, $13,500 for material costs and $6,000 for utility costs. How many pallets of each type of brick should be produced in that month to exactly utilize these allocations? Set up a system of linear equations, letting x, y, and z be the number of pallets of face, common, and refractory bricks, respectively, that must be produced in that month. DO NOT SOLVE THE SYSTEM.

15. A paper company produces high, medium, and low grade paper. The number of tons of each grade that is produced from one ton of pulp depends on the source of that pulp. The following table lists three sources and the amount of each grade of paper that can be made from one ton of pulp from each source.

|                | (Number of Tons) | | |
|                | High Grade | Medium Grade | Low Grade |
|----------------|------------|--------------|-----------|
| Brazilian Pulp | 0.6        | 0.2          | 0.2       |
| Domestic Pulp  | 0.5        | 0.2          | 0.3       |
| Recycled Pulp  | 0.3        | 0.3          | 0.4       |

The paper company has orders for 10 tons of high grade, 15 tons of medium grade, and 14 tons of low grade paper. How many tons of each type of pulp should be used to fill these orders exactly? Set up a system of linear equations, letting x, y, z be the number of tons of Brazilian pulp, domestic pulp, and recycled pulp, respectively, needed to fill the orders. DO NOT SOLVE THE SYSTEM.

16. A hospital dietician wants to insure that a certain meal consisting of rice, broccoli, and fish contains exactly 16,500 units of vitamin A, 3,150 units of vitamin E, and 6,020 units of vitamin C. One ounce of rice contains 500 units of vitamin A, 50 units of vitamin E, and 140 units of vitamin C. One ounce of broccoli contains 1000 units of vitamin A, 150 units of vitamin E, and 420 units of vitamin C. And one ounce of fish contains 1,000 units of vitamin A, 250 units of vitamin E, and 350 units of vitamin C. How many ounces of each food should this meal include? Set up a system of linear equations and solve using Gauss-Jordan elimination.

CHAPTER 5    Systems of Linear Equations; Matrices

17.  A trucking firm wants to purchase 10 trucks that will provide
     exactly 37 tons of additional shipping capacity.  A model A truck
     holds 3 tons, a model B truck holds 4 tons, and a model C truck
     holds 6 tons.  How many trucks of each model should the company
     purchase to provide the additional shipping capacity?  Set up a
     system of linear equations and solve using Gauss-Jordan elimination.

18.  Find:
$$-3 \begin{bmatrix} -1 & 0 & 1 \\ 4 & 1 & 0 \\ 0 & 1 & -1 \end{bmatrix} + \begin{bmatrix} -3 & 0 & 0 \\ 2 & 0 & 1 \\ -2 & -1 & -1 \end{bmatrix}$$

19.  Given $A = \begin{bmatrix} 1 \\ 1 \\ -1 \end{bmatrix}$ and $B = [1\ -3\ 0]$, find $AB$.

20.  Given $A = \begin{bmatrix} 1 & -4 & 0 \\ -3 & -1 & 0 \end{bmatrix}$ and $B = \begin{bmatrix} 1 & -4 \\ 0 & 1 \\ 4 & -1 \end{bmatrix}$, find $AB$.

21.  A retail company offers, through two different stores in a city,
     three models, A, B, and C, of a particular brand of tennis racket.
     The inventory of each model on hand in each store is summarized in
     matrix M.  Wholesale (W) and retail (R) prices of each model are
     summarized in matrix N.  Find the product MN and label its columns
     and rows appropriately.  What is the wholesale value of the inventory
     in Store 1?

$$M = \begin{matrix} & A & B & C \\ & \begin{bmatrix} 3 & 0 & 1 \\ 2 & 5 & 0 \end{bmatrix} & & \end{matrix} \begin{matrix} \text{Store 1} \\ \text{Store 2} \end{matrix} \qquad N = \begin{bmatrix} \$120 & \$180 \\ \$120 & \$150 \\ \$40 & \$50 \end{bmatrix} \begin{matrix} A \\ B \\ C \end{matrix}$$

CHAPTER 5    Systems of Linear Equations; Matrices

22. A supermarket chain sells oranges, apples, peaches, and bananas in three stores located throughout a large metropolitan area. The average number of pounds sold per day in each store is summarized in matrix M. "In season" and "out of season" prices, per pound, of each fruit are given in matrix N. What is the total, for the three stores, of "in season" daily revenue for the four fruits? The "out of season" peach sales represent what percentage of the daily total "out of season" revenues for Store 3?

$$M = \begin{array}{c} \\ \\ \\ \end{array} \begin{array}{cccc} \text{Fruit} \\ O & A & P & B \end{array}$$

$$M = \begin{bmatrix} 60 & 45 & 55 & 50 \\ 80 & 50 & 75 & 50 \\ 40 & 60 & 65 & 70 \end{bmatrix} \begin{array}{c} \text{Store 1} \\ \text{Store 2} \\ \text{Store 3} \end{array}$$

$$N = \begin{bmatrix} \$4.00 & \$7.00 \\ \$6.50 & \$9.50 \\ \$6.00 & \$6.00 \\ \$0.35 & \$0.60 \end{bmatrix} \begin{array}{c} O \\ A \\ P \\ B \end{array}$$

"In Season"    "Out of Season"

23. Use Gauss-Jordan elimination to find the inverse of $\begin{bmatrix} 1 & 1 \\ 2 & 3 \end{bmatrix}$.

24. Use Gauss-Jordan elimination, without introducing fractions, to find the inverse of $\begin{bmatrix} 4 & -2 & 3 \\ 0 & 1 & 0 \\ 1 & 0 & 1 \end{bmatrix}$.

25. The following message was encoded with the matrix $A = \begin{bmatrix} 1 & 1 \\ 3 & 4 \end{bmatrix}$. Decode this message.

28 92 32 123 37 132 34 118 17 56 42 141 35 117 36 117 46 165
27 96 39 137

26. Use $\begin{bmatrix} -5 & -4 \\ -1 & -1 \end{bmatrix}^{-1} = \begin{bmatrix} -1 & 4 \\ 1 & -5 \end{bmatrix}$ to solve: $\begin{aligned} -5x_1 - 4x_2 &= 2 \\ -x_1 - x_2 &= 1 \end{aligned}$

27. Use $\begin{bmatrix} -2 & -2 & 1 \\ 2 & 1 & 0 \\ 1 & 0 & 1 \end{bmatrix}^{-1} = \begin{bmatrix} 1 & 2 & -1 \\ -2 & -3 & 2 \\ -1 & -2 & 2 \end{bmatrix}$ to solve: $\begin{aligned} -2x_1 - 2x_2 + x_3 &= -1 \\ 2x_1 + x_2 &= 0 \\ x_1 + x_3 &= -2 \end{aligned}$

CHAPTER 5    Systems of Linear Equations; Matrices

28.  A chain of amusement parks pays experienced workers $240 per week
     and inexperienced workers $220 per week.  The total number of workers
     and the total weekly wages at three different parks are given in the
     table.  How many experienced workers does each park employ?  Set up
     a system of linear equations and solve using matrix inverse methods.

|                    | Park 1 | Park 2 | Park 3 |
|--------------------|--------|--------|--------|
| Number of workers  | 180    | 180    | 180    |
| Total weekly wages | 41,200 | 42,000 | 40,800 |

Key Sheet - CHAPTER 5

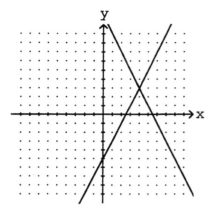

[1]  x = 4, y = 3

[2]  x = 2, y = -4

[3]  no solution

[4]  205 printers per month

[5]  (A)

[6]  (B)

[7]  $x_1 = -6$
     $x_2 = 8$
     $x_3 = 1$

[8]  $x_1 = -4$
     $x_2 = -3$
     $x_3 = 2$

[9]  $x_1 = -2$
     $x_2 = 3$

[10] $x_1 = -5s + 3$
     $x_2 = 2t - 1$
     $x_3 = s$
     $x_4 = t$
     s and t any real numbers

[11]   1,600 $5 seats
         800 $8 seats

---

[12]
$$x_1 + x_2 = 9{,}000$$
$$0.14x_1 + 0.07x_2 = 810$$

---

[13]
$$60x_1 + 40x_2 + 20x_3 = 60{,}000$$
$$70x_1 + 20x_2 + 40x_3 = 90{,}000$$
$$x_1 - 3x_3 = 0$$

---

[14]
$$60x + 60y + 85z = 11{,}500$$
$$70x + 55y + 95z = 13{,}500$$
$$35x + 30y + 45z = 6{,}000$$

---

[15]
$$0.6x + 0.5y + 0.3z = 10$$
$$0.2x + 0.2y + 0.3z = 15$$
$$0.2x + 0.3y + 0.4z = 14$$

---

[16]  5 ounces rice, 6 ounces broccoli, 8 ounces fish

---

[17]  3 model A, 7 model B, and 0 model C trucks; or
      5 model A, 4 model B, and 1 model C trucks; or
      7 model A, 1 model B, and 2 model C trucks

---

[18]
$$\begin{bmatrix} 0 & 4 & -3 \\ -10 & -3 & 1 \\ -2 & -4 & 2 \end{bmatrix}$$

---

[19]
$$\begin{bmatrix} 1 & -3 & 0 \\ 1 & -3 & 0 \\ -1 & 3 & 0 \end{bmatrix}$$

---

[20]
$$\begin{bmatrix} 4 & -5 \\ -3 & 11 \end{bmatrix}$$

---

[21]
$$\begin{bmatrix} \$400 & \$590 \\ \$840 & \$1110 \end{bmatrix} \begin{matrix} \text{Store 1} \\ \text{Store 2} \end{matrix} \qquad \$400$$

with column headings W   R

---

[22]  $2957;   30.42%

---

[23]
$$\begin{bmatrix} 3 & -1 \\ -2 & 1 \end{bmatrix}$$

---

[24]
$$\begin{bmatrix} 1 & 2 & -3 \\ 0 & 1 & 0 \\ -1 & -2 & 4 \end{bmatrix}$$

---

[25]  THE PURPLE OWL IS LOST

## Key Sheet - CHAPTER 5

[26]
$x_1 = 2$
$x_2 = -3$

---

[27]
$x_1 = 1$
$x_2 = -2$
$x_3 = -3$

---

[28]
Park 1: 80 experienced workers
Park 2: 120 experienced workers
Park 3: 60 experienced workers

---

Essentials of College Mathematics, Third Edition
Raymond A. Barnett and Michael R. Ziegler

---

CHAPTER 5    Systems of Linear Equations; Matrices

---

1.  Solve graphically:  $x + y = 0$
    $3x - 2y = -20$

2.  Solve by elimination using addition: $2x - 4y = -20$
    $3x + 4y = 10$

3.  Solve by elimination using addition:  $8x - 10y = 6$
    $12x - 15y = -9$

4.  A company that manufactures laser printers for computers has monthly fixed costs of \$135,000 and variable costs of \$750 per unit produced.  The company sells the printers for \$1,250 per unit. How many printers must be sold each month for the company to break even?

5.  Only one of the following augmented matrices of a linear system is in a reduced form.  Indicate by letter which one.

    (A) $\begin{bmatrix} 1 & 0 & | & -1 \\ 0 & 0 & | & 0 \\ 0 & 1 & | & 5 \end{bmatrix}$  (B) $\begin{bmatrix} 1 & -5 & 0 & | & 4 \\ 0 & 0 & 1 & | & -4 \\ 0 & 0 & 0 & | & 0 \end{bmatrix}$  (C) $\begin{bmatrix} 0 & 1 & | & 3 \\ 1 & 0 & | & -2 \end{bmatrix}$  (D) $\begin{bmatrix} 1 & 0 & 3 & | & -5 \\ 0 & 0 & 1 & | & 2 \end{bmatrix}$

6.  The reduced forms for three systems of equations are given below. Indicate by letter which system has no solution.

    (A) $\begin{bmatrix} 1 & 3 & 0 & | & 4 \\ 0 & 0 & 1 & | & -3 \\ 0 & 0 & 0 & | & 0 \end{bmatrix}$  (B) $\begin{bmatrix} 1 & 0 & | & 2 \\ 0 & 1 & | & 4 \\ 0 & 0 & | & 0 \end{bmatrix}$  (C) $\begin{bmatrix} 1 & 0 & 2 & | & 4 \\ 0 & 1 & 4 & | & 3 \\ 0 & 0 & 0 & | & 1 \end{bmatrix}$

7.  Solve the linear system corresponding to the following augmented matrix:

    $\begin{bmatrix} 1 & 0 & 5 & | & 2 \\ 0 & 1 & 1 & | & -3 \\ 0 & 0 & 0 & | & 0 \end{bmatrix}$

8.  Solve by augmented matrix methods using Gauss-Jordan elimination:

    $x_1 - 3x_2 - 3x_3 = -4$
    $x_2 - 4x_3 = 15$
    $x_1 \quad + x_3 = -7$

## CHAPTER 5    Systems of Linear Equations; Matrices

9.  Solve by augmented matrix methods using Gauss-Jordan elimination:

$$2x_1 + 2x_2 = -2$$
$$4x_1 - 2x_2 = 14$$
$$x_1 + x_2 = -1$$

10. Solve by augmented matrix methods using Gauss-Jordan elimination:

$$x_1 + x_2 + 3x_3 - x_4 = 8$$
$$x_1 - x_2 + 3x_3 + x_4 = 10$$

11. A performance center has 2,200 seats. Tickets for an event are $5 and $10 per seat. Assuming that all tickets are sold and bring in a total of $16,500, how many of each type of ticket were sold? Set up a system of equations and solve by augmented matrix methods using Gauss-Jordan elimination.

12. If $7,000 is to be invested, part at 13% and the rest at 7%, how much should be invested at each rate so that the total annual return will be the same as $7,000 invested at 9%? Set up a system of linear equations, letting $x_1$ be the amount invested at 13% and $x_2$ be the amount invested at 7%. DO NOT SOLVE THE SYSTEM.

13. Unit labor and material costs for manufacturing each of three types of products M, N, and P are given in the table:

|           | Product |      |      |
|-----------|---------|------|------|
|           | M       | N    | P    |
| Labor     | $20     | $20  | $40  |
| Materials | $30     | $50  | $60  |

The weekly allocation for labor is $30,000 and for materials is $60,000. There are to be 4 times as many units of product M manufactured as units of product P. How many of each type of product should be manufactured each week to use exactly each of the weekly allocations? Set up a system of linear equations, letting $x_1$, $x_2$, and $x_3$ be the number of units of products M, N, and P, respectively, manufactured in one week. DO NOT SOLVE THE SYSTEM.

---

CHAPTER 5    Systems of Linear Equations; Matrices

---

14. In producing three types of bricks: face bricks, common bricks, and refractory bricks, a factory incurs labor, material, and utility costs. To produce one pallet of face bricks, the labor, material, and utility costs are $55, $90, and $40, respectively. To produce one pallet of common bricks, the labor, material, and utility costs are $55, $75, and $35, respectively, while the corresponding costs for refractory bricks are $80, $115, and $50. In a certain month the company has allocated $12,000 for labor costs, $14,000 for material costs and $5,500 for utility costs. How many pallets of each type of brick should be produced in that month to exactly utilize these allocations? Set up a system of linear equations, letting x, y, and z be the number of pallets of face, common, and refractory bricks, respectively, that must be produced in that month. DO NOT SOLVE THE SYSTEM.

15. A paper company produces high, medium, and low grade paper. The number of tons of each grade that is produced from one ton of pulp depends on the source of that pulp. The following table lists three sources and the amount of each grade of paper that can be made from one ton of pulp from each source.

|                | (Number of Tons) | | |
|                | High Grade | Medium Grade | Low Grade |
|----------------|------------|--------------|-----------|
| Brazilian Pulp | 0.7        | 0.2          | 0.1       |
| Domestic Pulp  | 0.6        | 0.2          | 0.2       |
| Recycled Pulp  | 0.4        | 0.3          | 0.3       |

The paper company has orders for 12 tons of high grade, 15 tons of medium grade, and 14 tons of low grade paper. How many tons of each type of pulp should be used to fill these orders exactly? Set up a system of linear equations, letting x, y, z be the number of tons of Brazilian pulp, domestic pulp, and recycled pulp, respectively, needed to fill the orders. DO NOT SOLVE THE SYSTEM.

16. A hospital dietician wants to insure that a certain meal consisting of rice, broccoli, and fish contains exactly 26,400 units of vitamin A, 1,320 units of vitamin E, and 4,020 units of vitamin C. One ounce of rice contains 400 units of vitamin A, 30 units of vitamin E, and 120 units of vitamin C. One ounce of broccoli contains 800 units of vitamin A, 90 units of vitamin E, and 360 units of vitamin C. And one ounce of fish contains 2,800 units of vitamin A, 90 units of vitamin E, and 180 units of vitamin C. How many ounces of each food should this meal include? Set up a system of linear equations and solve using Gauss-Jordan elimination.

CHAPTER 5    Systems of Linear Equations; Matrices

17. A trucking firm wants to purchase 13 trucks that will provide
    exactly 34 tons of additional shipping capacity.  A model A truck
    holds 2 tons, a model B truck holds 3 tons, and a model C truck
    holds 5 tons.  How many trucks of each model should the company
    purchase to provide the additional shipping capacity?  Set up a
    system of linear equations and solve using Gauss-Jordan elimination.

18. Find: $-4 \begin{bmatrix} -1 & 0 & 1 \\ 2 & 1 & 0 \\ 0 & 1 & -1 \end{bmatrix} + \begin{bmatrix} 3 & 0 & 0 \\ -4 & 0 & 1 \\ -2 & -1 & -1 \end{bmatrix}$

19. Given $A = \begin{bmatrix} 4 \\ 1 \\ -1 \end{bmatrix}$ and $B = [1 \ 4 \ 0]$, find AB.

20. Given $A = \begin{bmatrix} 1 & -1 & 0 \\ 3 & -1 & 0 \end{bmatrix}$ and $B = \begin{bmatrix} 1 & -4 \\ 0 & 1 \\ -2 & -1 \end{bmatrix}$, find AB.

21. A retail company offers, through two different stores in a city,
    three models, A, B, and C, of a particular brand of inflatable boat.
    The inventory of each model on hand in each store is summarized in
    matrix M.  Wholesale (W) and retail (R) prices of each model are
    summarized in matrix N.  Find the product MN and label its columns
    and rows appropriately.  What is the wholesale value of the inventory
    in Store 1?

$$M = \begin{bmatrix} 2 & 0 & 1 \\ 4 & 4 & 0 \end{bmatrix} \begin{matrix} \text{Store 1} \\ \text{Store 2} \end{matrix} \qquad N = \begin{bmatrix} \$ \ 80 & \$120 \\ \$ \ 40 & \$ \ 50 \\ \$ \ 80 & \$100 \end{bmatrix} \begin{matrix} A \\ B \\ C \end{matrix}$$

with column labels A B C over M and W R over N.

CHAPTER 5    Systems of Linear Equations; Matrices

22. A supermarket chain sells oranges, apples, peaches, and bananas in three stores located throughout a large metropolitan area.  The average number of pounds sold per day in each store is summarized in matrix M.  "In season" and "out of season" prices, per pound, of each fruit are given in matrix N.  What is the total, for the three stores, of "in season" daily revenue for the four fruits? The "out of season" peach sales represent what percentage of the daily total "out of season" revenues for Store 3?

$$M = \begin{bmatrix} O & A & P & B \\ 40 & 80 & 70 & 50 \\ 60 & 90 & 55 & 45 \\ 65 & 40 & 70 & 80 \end{bmatrix} \begin{matrix} \\ \text{Store 1} \\ \text{Store 2} \\ \text{Store 3} \end{matrix}$$

Fruit

$$N = \begin{bmatrix} \text{"In Season"} & \text{"Out of Season"} \\ \$3.00 & \$8.00 \\ \$6.00 & \$9.50 \\ \$6.00 & \$3.50 \\ \$0.35 & \$0.50 \end{bmatrix} \begin{matrix} O \\ A \\ P \\ B \end{matrix}$$

23. Use Gauss-Jordan elimination to find the inverse of $\begin{bmatrix} -1 & 1 \\ 8 & -9 \end{bmatrix}$.

24. Use Gauss-Jordan elimination, without introducing fractions, to find the inverse of $\begin{bmatrix} -2 & 3 & -3 \\ 0 & 1 & 0 \\ 1 & 0 & 1 \end{bmatrix}$.

25. The following message was encoded with the matrix $A = \begin{bmatrix} 1 & 1 \\ 5 & 6 \end{bmatrix}$ Decode this message.

    28 148 32 187 31 164 27 147 25 145 31 159 22 117 36 189
    46 257 22 125 19 100

26. Use $\begin{bmatrix} 3 & -2 \\ -1 & 1 \end{bmatrix}^{-1} = \begin{bmatrix} 1 & 2 \\ 1 & 3 \end{bmatrix}$ to solve: $\begin{aligned} 3x_1 - 2x_2 &= -4 \\ -x_1 + x_2 &= -4 \end{aligned}$

27. Use $\begin{bmatrix} -3 & 1 & -5 \\ 1 & 1 & 0 \\ 1 & 0 & 1 \end{bmatrix}^{-1} = \begin{bmatrix} 1 & -1 & 5 \\ -1 & 2 & -5 \\ -1 & 1 & -4 \end{bmatrix}$ to solve: $\begin{aligned} -3x_1 + x_2 - 5x_3 &= 1 \\ x_1 + x_2 &= 0 \\ x_1 + x_3 &= 3 \end{aligned}$

CHAPTER 5    Systems of Linear Equations; Matrices

28.  A chain of amusement parks pays experienced workers $300 per week
     and inexperienced workers $250 per week.  The total number of workers
     and the total weekly wages at three different parks are given in the
     table.  How many experienced workers does each park employ?  Set up
     a system of linear equations and solve using matrix inverse methods.

|                    | Park 1 | Park 2 | Park 3  |
|--------------------|--------|--------|---------|
| Number of workers  | 300    | 250    | 450     |
| Total weekly wages | 85,000 | 65,000 | 120,000 |

Key Sheet - CHAPTER 5

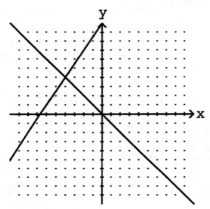

[1]  x = -4, y = 4

[2]  x = -2, y = 4

[3]  no solution

[4]  270 printers per month

[5]  (B)

[6]  (C)

$x_1 = -5t + 2$
$x_2 = -t - 3$
$x_3 = t$
[7]  t = any real number

$x_1 = -4$
$x_2 = 3$
[8]  $x_3 = -3$

$x_1 = 2$
[9]  $x_2 = -3$

$x_1 = -3s + 9$
$x_2 = t - 1$
$x_3 = s$
$x_4 = t$
[10] s and t any real numbers

Key Sheet - CHAPTER 5

[11] 1,100 $5 seats
1,100 $10 seats

[12]
$$x_1 + x_2 = 7,000$$
$$0.13x_1 + 0.07x_2 = 630$$

[13]
$$20x_1 + 20x_2 + 40x_3 = 30,000$$
$$30x_1 + 50x_2 + 60x_3 = 60,000$$
$$x_1 - 4x_3 = 0$$

[14]
$$55x + 55y + 80z = 12,000$$
$$90x + 75y + 115z = 14,000$$
$$40x + 35y + 50z = 5,500$$

[15]
$$0.7x + 0.6y + 0.4z = 12$$
$$0.2x + 0.2y + 0.3z = 15$$
$$0.1x + 0.2y + 0.3z = 14$$

[16] 5 ounces rice, 6 ounces broccoli, 7 ounces fish

[17] 5 model A, 8 model B, and 0 model C trucks; or
7 model A, 5 model B, and 1 model C trucks; or
9 model A, 2 model B, and 2 model C trucks

[18]
$$\begin{bmatrix} 7 & 3 & -4 \\ -12 & -4 & 1 \\ -2 & -5 & 3 \end{bmatrix}$$

[19]
$$\begin{bmatrix} 4 & 16 & 0 \\ 1 & 4 & 0 \\ -1 & -4 & 0 \end{bmatrix}$$

[20]
$$\begin{bmatrix} -2 & -2 \\ 3 & -13 \end{bmatrix}$$

[21]
$$\begin{bmatrix} W & R \\ \$240 & \$340 \\ \$480 & \$680 \end{bmatrix}$$ Store 1    $240
Store 2

[22] $2986.25;   20.68%

[23]
$$\begin{bmatrix} -9 & -1 \\ -8 & -1 \end{bmatrix}$$

[24]
$$\begin{bmatrix} 1 & -3 & 3 \\ 0 & 1 & 0 \\ -1 & 3 & -2 \end{bmatrix}$$

[25] THE VIOLET DOG IS GONE

## Key Sheet - CHAPTER 5

[26] $x_1 = -12$
$x_2 = -16$

[27] $x_1 = 16$
$x_2 = -16$
$x_3 = -13$

[28] Park 1: 200 experienced workers
Park 2: 50 experienced workers
Park 3: 150 experienced workers

Essentials of College Mathematics, Third Edition
Raymond A. Barnett and Michael R. Ziegler

CHAPTER 6    Linear Inequalities and Linear Programming

1.    Graph: $6x - 4y \geq 24$

2.    Solve the following system graphically: $x \leq -3$
      $y > 3$
      $4x + 2y < 16$

3.    Find the coordinates of the corner points of the solution region for:
      $4x + 3y \geq 72$
      $x + 5y \leq 35$
      $x \geq 0$
      $y \geq 0$

4.    Formulate the following problem as a linear programming problem (DO
      NOT SOLVE):
      A small accounting firm prepares tax returns for two types of
      customers: individuals and small businesses.  Data is collected during
      an interview.  A computer system is used to produce the tax return.
      It takes 2.5 hours to enter data into the computer for an individual
      tax return and 4 hours to enter data for a small business tax
      return.  There is a maximum of 45 hours per week for data entry.  It
      takes 20 minutes for the computer to process an individual tax return
      and 30 minutes to process a small business tax return.  The computer
      is available for a maximum of 1,050 minutes per week.  The accounting
      firm makes a profit of $225 on each individual tax return processed
      and a profit of $300 on each small business tax return processed.
      How many of each type of tax return should the firm schedule each
      week in order to maximize its profit?  (Let $x_1$ equal the number of
      individual tax returns and $x_2$ the number of small business tax
      returns.)

5.    Formulate the following problem as a linear programming problem (DO
      NOT SOLVE):
      A company which produces three kinds of spaghetti sauce has two
      plants.  The East plant produces 5,500 jars of plain sauce, 1,000 jars
      of sauce with mushrooms, and 6,500 jars of hot spicy sauce per day.
      The West plant produces 4,500 jars of plain sauce, 4,000 jars of sauce
      with mushrooms, and 3,500 jars of hot spicy sauce per day.  The cost
      to operate the East plant is $6,000 per day and the cost to operate
      the West plant is $6,500 per day.  How many days should each plant
      operate to minimize cost and to fill an order for at least 9,000 jars
      of plain sauce, 7,000 jars of sauce with mushrooms, and 6,000 jars of
      hot spicy sauce?  (Let $x_1$ equal the number of days East plant should
      operate and $x_2$ the number of days West plant should operate.)

CHAPTER 6    Linear Inequalities and Linear Programming

6.  Formulate the following problem as a linear programming problem
    (DO NOT SOLVE):
    A steel company produces two types of machine dies, part A and
    part B.  Part A requires 6 hours of casting time and 2 hours of
    firing time.  Part B requires 7 hours of casting time and 3 hours
    of firing time.  The maximum number of hours per week available for
    casting and firing are 80 and 75, respectively.  The company makes
    a $7.00 profit on each part A that it produces, and a $3.00 profit
    on each part B that it produces. How many of each type should the
    company produce each week in order to maximize its profit?  (Let
    $x_1$ equal the number of A parts and $x_2$ equal the number of B parts
    produced each week.)

7.  Formulate the following problem as a linear programming problem
    (DO NOT SOLVE):
    A dietician can purchase an ounce of chicken for $0.12 and an
    ounce of potatoes for $0.06.  Each ounce of chicken contains 13
    units of protein and 22 units of carbohydrates.  Each ounce of
    potatoes contains 7 units of protein and 27 units of
    carbohydrates.  The minimum daily requirements for the patients
    under the dietician's care are 42 units of protein and 62 units of
    carbohydrates.  How many ounces of each type of food should the
    dietician purchase for each patient so as to minimize costs and at
    the same time insure the minimum daily requirements of protein and
    carbohydrates?  (Let $x_1$ equal the number of ounces of chicken and $x_2$
    the number of ounces of potatoes purchased per patient.)

8.  A vineyard produces two special wines, a white, and a red.  A
    bottle of the white wine requires 4 pounds of grapes and 1 hour
    of processing time.  A bottle of the red wine requires 5 pounds
    of grapes and 2 hours of processing time.  The vineyard has on hand
    788 pounds of grapes and can allot 200 hours of processing time to
    the production of these wines.  A bottle of the white wine sells for
    $16.00, while a bottle of the red wine sells for $30.00.  How
    many bottles of each type should the vineyard produce in order to
    maximize gross sales?  (Solve using the geometric method.)

---

CHAPTER 6   Linear Inequalities and Linear Programming

---

9.  Solve the following linear programming problem by determining the feasible region on the graph below and testing the corner points:
Minimize $C = x_1 + 6x_2$

Subject to $2x_1 + 3x_2 \geq 30$

$4x_1 + x_2 \leq 20$

$x_1, x_2 \geq 0$

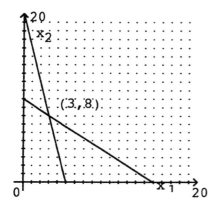

10. The corner points for the bounded feasible region determined by the system of inequalities:

$5x_1 + x_2 \leq 35$

$3x_1 + 4x_2 \leq 72$

$x_1, x_2 \geq 0$

are  $O = (0, 0)$, $A = (0, 18)$, $B = (4, 15)$ and $C = (7, 0)$.  Find the optimal solution for the objective profit function:
$P = 5x_1 + 5x_2$

11. A basic solution for the system:

$3x_1 + 5x_2 + s_1 \qquad = 75$

$x_1 + 4x_2 \qquad + s_2 = 32$

is $x_1 = 20$, $x_2 = 3$, $s_1 = 0$, $s_2 = 0$.

Identify the basic and nonbasic variables and determine if the solution is feasible or not feasible.

CHAPTER 6    Linear Inequalities and Linear Programming

12. For the following linear system associated with a linear programming problem, find the value of the basic variables and determine if the basic solution is feasible:

$$4x_1 + 5x_2 + s_1 \quad\quad = 80$$
$$3x_1 + \ x_2 \quad\quad + s_2 = 27$$

if $x_1$ and $s_1$ are chosen as nonbasic variables.

13. Using slack variables, write the initial system for the following linear programming problem:

Maximize $P = 20x_1 - 10x_2$

Subject to $6x_1 + 8x_2 \le 20$
$$x_1 + 7x_2 \le 25$$
$$8x_1 - \ x_2 \le 25$$
$$x_1,\ x_2 \ge 0$$

14. Write the basic solution for the following simplex tableau:

$$
\begin{array}{ccccccc|c}
x_1 & x_2 & x_3 & s_1 & s_2 & s_3 & P & \\
0 & 0 & 9 & 1 & 0 & 0 & 0 & 27 \\
1 & -6 & 10 & 0 & 0 & 1 & 0 & 24 \\
0 & 9 & 6 & 0 & 1 & 1 & 0 & 20 \\
\hline
0 & -8 & -7 & 0 & 0 & 4 & 1 & 50
\end{array}
$$

15. Write the simplex tableau, label the columns and rows, circle the pivot element, and identify the entering and exiting variables for the linear programming problem:

Maximize $P = 6x_1 + 3x_2$

Subject to $3x_1 + 4x_2 \le 6$
$$7x_2 \le 3$$
$$3x_1 + 6x_2 \le 7$$
$$-4x_1 + 7x_2 \le 16$$
$$x_1,\ x_2 \ge 0$$

16. Perform the next pivot operation on the following simplex tableau and write the resulting tableau:

$$
\begin{array}{cccccc|c}
0 & 0 & 5 & 0 & 1 & 0 & 15 \\
5 & 0 & 2 & 1 & 0 & 0 & 8 \\
-2 & 1 & 2 & 0 & 0 & 0 & 4 \\
\hline
-3 & 0 & -9 & 0 & 0 & 1 & 35
\end{array}
$$

## CHAPTER 6    Linear Inequalities and Linear Programming

17. State whether the optimal solution has been found, an additional
    pivot is required, or there is no solution for the problem
    corresponding to the following simplex tableau:

$$
\begin{array}{ccccccc}
x_1 & x_2 & x_3 & s_1 & s_2 & s_3 & P \\
\end{array}
$$

$$
\left[\begin{array}{ccccccc|c}
-1 & 0 & 0 & 3 & 1 & 1 & 0 & 8 \\
0 & 1 & 0 & -2 & 0 & 0 & 0 & 20 \\
-3 & 0 & 1 & 2 & 1 & 0 & 0 & 5 \\
\hline
2 & 0 & 0 & 3 & 2 & 0 & 1 & 52
\end{array}\right]
$$

18. Solve the following linear programming problem using the simplex
    method:

    Maximize $P = x_1 - x_2$

    Subject to $x_1 + x_2 \le 6$

    $\qquad\qquad 3x_1 + 10x_2 \le 30$

    $\qquad\qquad\qquad x_1,\ x_2 \ge 0$

Key Sheet - CHAPTER 6

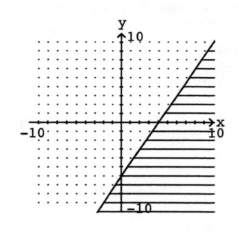

[1] _____

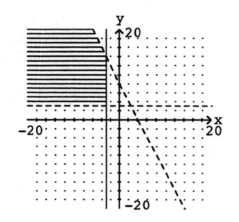

[2] _____

[3]   (18, 0), (35, 0), (15, 4)
_____

    Maximize P = $225x_1$ + $300x_2$
    Subject to $2.5x_1$ + $4x_2$ ≤ 45
              $20x_1$ + $30x_2$ ≤ 1,050
[4]                $x_1$, $x_2$ ≥ 0
_____

    Minimize C = $6,000x_1$ + $6,500x_2$
    Subject to $5,500x_1$ + $4,500x_2$ ≥ 9,000
              $1,000x_1$ + $4,000x_2$ ≥ 7,000
              $6,500x_1$ + $3,500x_2$ ≥ 6,000
[5]                $x_1$, $x_2$ ≥ 0
_____

## Key Sheet - CHAPTER 6

[6]
Maximize $P = 7x_1 + 3x_2$
Subject to $6x_1 + 7x_2 \leq 80$
$2x_1 + 3x_2 \leq 75$
$x_1, x_2 \geq 0$

[7]
Minimize $C = 0.12x_1 + 0.06x_2$
Subject to $13x_1 + 7x_2 \geq 42$
$22x_1 + 27x_2 \geq 62$
$x_1, x_2 \geq 0$

[8] 192 bottles of white wine, and 4 bottles of red wine

[9] Minimum at (3, 8)

[10] Maximum occurs at (4, 15) and is 95.

[11]
Basic variables: $x_1, x_2$
Nonbasic variables: $s_1, s_2$
Solution is feasible.

[12]
$x_2 = 16$, $s_2 = 11$
The basic solution is feasible.

[13]
$6x_1 + 8x_2 + s_1 \qquad\qquad\qquad = 20$
$x_1 + 7x_2 \qquad + s_2 \qquad\qquad = 25$
$8x_1 - x_2 \qquad\qquad + s_3 \qquad = 25$
$-20x_1 + 10x_2 \qquad\qquad\qquad + P = 0$
$x_1, x_2 \geq 0$
$s_1, s_2, s_3 \geq 0$

[14] $x_1 = 24$, $x_2 = 0$, $x_3 = 0$, $s_1 = 27$, $s_2 = 20$, $s_3 = 0$, $P = 50$

[15]

|  |  | Enter |  |  |  |  |  |  |  |
|------|------|-----|-----|-----|-----|-----|-----|-----|-----|
|  |  | $x_1$ | $x_2$ | $s_1$ | $s_2$ | $s_3$ | $s_4$ | $P$ |  |
| Exit | $s_1$ | (3) | 4 | 1 | 0 | 0 | 0 | 0 | 6 |
|  | $s_2$ | 0 | 7 | 0 | 1 | 0 | 0 | 0 | 3 |
|  | $s_3$ | 3 | 6 | 0 | 0 | 1 | 0 | 0 | 7 |
|  | $s_4$ | -4 | 7 | 0 | 0 | 0 | 1 | 0 | 16 |
|  |  | -6 | -3 | 0 | 0 | 0 | 0 | 1 | 0 |

## Key Sheet - CHAPTER 6

[16]
$$\begin{bmatrix} 5 & -\frac{5}{2} & 0 & 0 & 1 & 0 & 5 \\ 7 & -1 & 0 & 1 & 0 & 0 & 4 \\ -1 & \frac{1}{2} & 1 & 0 & 0 & 0 & 2 \\ \hline -12 & \frac{9}{2} & 0 & 0 & 0 & 1 & 53 \end{bmatrix}$$

[17] Optimal solution has been found.

[18] Max P = 6 at $x_1$ = 6 and $x_2$ = 0

CHAPTER 6   Linear Inequalities and Linear Programming

1.   Graph: $7x - 2y \leq 14$

2.   Solve the following system graphically: $x \leq -2$
                                             $y > 2$
                                             $3x + 3y < 18$

3.   Find the coordinates of the corner points of the solution region for:
     $3x + y \leq 21$
     $2x + 5y \geq 40$
     $x \geq 0$
     $y \geq 0$

4.   Formulate the following problem as a linear programming problem (DO
     NOT SOLVE):
     A small accounting firm prepares tax returns for two types of
     customers: individuals and small businesses.  Data is collected during
     an interview.  A computer system is used to produce the tax return.
     It takes 2.5 hours to enter data into the computer for an individual
     tax return and 4 hours to enter data for a small business tax
     return.  There is a maximum of 40 hours per week for data entry.  It
     takes 20 minutes for the computer to process an individual tax return
     and 30 minutes to process a small business tax return.  The computer
     is available for a maximum of 1,050 minutes per week.  The accounting
     firm makes a profit of $175 on each individual tax return processed
     and a profit of $275 on each small business tax return processed.
     How many of each type of tax return should the firm schedule each
     week in order to maximize its profit?  (Let $x_1$ equal the number of
     individual tax returns and $x_2$ the number of small business tax
     returns.)

5.   Formulate the following problem as a linear programming problem (DO
     NOT SOLVE):
     A company which produces three kinds of spaghetti sauce has two
     plants.  The East plant produces 3,000 jars of plain sauce, 6,000 jars
     of sauce with mushrooms, and 4,500 jars of hot spicy sauce per day.
     The West plant produces 2,000 jars of plain sauce, 5,500 jars of sauce
     with mushrooms, and 2,500 jars of hot spicy sauce per day.  The cost
     to operate the East plant is $9,500 per day and the cost to operate
     the West plant is $7,000 per day.  How many days should each plant
     operate to minimize cost and to fill an order for at least 6,500 jars
     of plain sauce, 8,500 jars of sauce with mushrooms, and 8,000 jars of
     hot spicy sauce?  (Let $x_1$ equal the number of days East plant should
     operate and $x_2$ the number of days West plant should operate.)

CHAPTER 6    Linear Inequalities and Linear Programming

6.  Formulate the following problem as a linear programming problem
    (DO NOT SOLVE):
    A steel company produces two types of machine dies, part A and
    part B.  Part A requires 2 hours of casting time and 5 hours of
    firing time.  Part B requires 8 hours of casting time and 7 hours
    of firing time.  The maximum number of hours per week available for
    casting and firing are 90 and 95, respectively.  The company makes
    a $4.00 profit on each part A that it produces, and a $7.00 profit
    on each part B that it produces.  How many of each type should the
    company produce each week in order to maximize its profit?  (Let
    $x_1$ equal the number of A parts and $x_2$ equal the number of B parts

    produced each week.)

7.  Formulate the following problem as a linear programming problem
    (DO NOT SOLVE):
    A dietician can purchase an ounce of chicken for $0.23 and an
    ounce of potatoes for $0.02.  Each ounce of chicken contains 13
    units of protein and 19 units of carbohydrates.  Each ounce of
    potatoes contains 5 units of protein and 31 units of
    carbohydrates.  The minimum daily requirements for the patients
    under the dietician's care are 44 units of protein and 55 units of
    carbohydrates.  How many ounces of each type of food should the
    dietician purchase for each patient so as to minimize costs and at
    the same time insure the minimum daily requirements of protein and
    carbohydrates?  (Let $x_1$ equal the number of ounces of chicken and $x_2$

    the number of ounces of potatoes purchased per patient.)

8.  A vineyard produces two special wines, a white, and a red.  A
    bottle of the white wine requires 12 pounds of grapes and 1 hour
    of processing time.  A bottle of the red wine requires 21 pounds
    of grapes and 2 hours of processing time.  The vineyard has on hand
    1,764 pounds of grapes and can allot 150 hours of processing time to
    the production of these wines.  A bottle of the white wine sells for
    $16.00, while a bottle of the red wine sells for $30.00.  How
    many bottles of each type should the vineyard produce in order to
    maximize gross sales?  (Solve using the geometric method.)

CHAPTER 6    Linear Inequalities and Linear Programming

9.    Solve the following linear programming problem by determining the
      feasible region on the graph below and testing the corner points:
      Maximize $P = x_1 + 6x_2$
      Subject to   $x_1 + 3x_2 \leq 18$
      $$4x_1 + 2x_2 \geq 32$$
      $$x_1, x_2 \geq 0$$

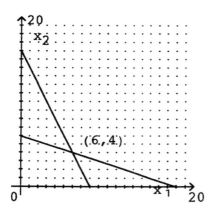

10.   The corner points for the bounded feasible region determined by the
      system of inequalities:
      $5x_1 + 4x_2 \leq 80$
      $x_1 + 3x_2 \leq 27$
      $x_1, x_2 \geq 0$
      are  $O = (0, 0)$, $A = (0, 9)$, $B = (12, 5)$ and $C = (16, 0)$.  Find the
      optimal solution for the objective profit function:
      $P = 5x_1 + 5x_2$

11.   A basic solution for the system:
      $4x_1 + 2x_2 + s_1 \quad = 64$
      $5x_1 + 3x_2 \quad + s_2 = 90$
      is $x_1 = 16$, $x_2 = 0$, $s_1 = 0$, $s_2 = 10$.
      Identify the basic and nonbasic variables and determine if the
      solution is feasible or not feasible.

CHAPTER 6   Linear Inequalities and Linear Programming

12. For the following linear system associated with a linear programming problem, find the value of the basic variables and determine if the basic solution is feasible:

$$5x_1 + 3x_2 + s_1 \quad\quad = 75$$
$$x_1 + 4x_2 \quad\quad + s_2 = 32$$

if $s_1$ and $s_2$ are chosen as nonbasic variables.

13. Using slack variables, write the initial system for the following linear programming problem:

Maximize $P = 25x_1 - 30x_2$

Subject to $5x_1 + 8x_2 \le 25$
$$9x_1 + 6x_2 \le 30$$
$$8x_1 - 9x_2 \le 30$$
$$x_1, \; x_2 \ge 0$$

14. Write the basic solution for the following simplex tableau:

$$
\begin{array}{ccccccc|c}
x_1 & x_2 & x_3 & s_1 & s_2 & s_3 & P & \\
\hline
0 & 5 & 9 & 0 & 1 & 1 & 0 & 6 \\
1 & -9 & 3 & 0 & 0 & 1 & 0 & 36 \\
0 & 0 & 5 & 1 & 0 & 0 & 0 & 15 \\
\hline
0 & -6 & -8 & 0 & 0 & 4 & 1 & 40
\end{array}
$$

15. Write the simplex tableau, label the columns and rows, circle the pivot element, and identify the entering and exiting variables for the linear programming problem:

Maximize $P = 8x_1 + 5x_2$

Subject to $-x_1 + 7x_2 \le 4$
$$7x_2 \le 5$$
$$5x_1 + 8x_2 \le 9$$
$$5x_1 + \; x_2 \le 8$$
$$x_1, \; x_2 \ge 0$$

16. Perform the next pivot operation on the following simplex tableau and write the resulting tableau:

$$
\begin{bmatrix}
0 & 0 & 3 & 0 & 1 & 0 & 9 \\
-4 & 1 & 4 & 0 & 0 & 0 & 8 \\
3 & 0 & 4 & 1 & 0 & 0 & 16 \\
\hline
-7 & 0 & -8 & 0 & 0 & 1 & 40
\end{bmatrix}
$$

CHAPTER 6    Linear Inequalities and Linear Programming

17.  State whether the optimal solution has been found, an additional
     pivot is required, or there is no solution for the problem
     corresponding to the following simplex tableau:

$$\begin{array}{ccccccc}
x_1 & x_2 & x_3 & s_1 & s_2 & s_3 & P \\
\end{array}$$

$$\left[\begin{array}{ccccccc|c}
1 & 0 & 0 & 3 & 1 & 1 & 0 & 8 \\
0 & 1 & 0 & -2 & 0 & 0 & 0 & 20 \\
-1 & 0 & 1 & 2 & 1 & 0 & 0 & 5 \\
\hline
-2 & 0 & 0 & 2 & 2 & 0 & 1 & 50
\end{array}\right]$$

18.  Solve the following linear programming problem using the simplex
     method:

     Maximize $P = -x_1 + x_2$

     Subject to $x_1 + x_2 \leq 2$

     $x_1 + 4x_2 \leq 4$

     $x_1,\ x_2 \geq 0$

Key Sheet - CHAPTER 6

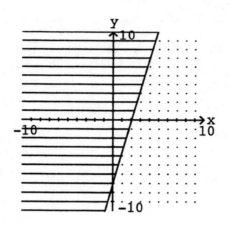

[1]

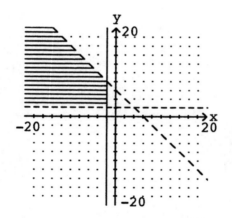

[2]

[3]  (0, 21), (0, 8), (5, 6)

Maximize P = $175x_1 + 275x_2$
Subject to $2.5x_1 + 4x_2 \le 40$
$\qquad\quad 20x_1 + 30x_2 \le 1,050$
[4] $\qquad\qquad x_1,\ x_2 \ge 0$

Minimize C = $9,500x_1 + 7,000x_2$
Subject to $3,000x_1 + 2,000x_2 \ge 6,500$
$\qquad\quad 6,000x_1 + 5,500x_2 \ge 8,500$
$\qquad\quad 4,500x_1 + 2,500x_2 \ge 8,000$
[5] $\qquad\qquad x_1,\ x_2 \ge 0$

## Key Sheet - CHAPTER 6

[6]
Maximize $P = 4x_1 + 7x_2$
Subject to $2x_1 + 8x_2 \le 90$
$5x_1 + 7x_2 \le 95$
$x_1, x_2 \ge 0$

[7]
Minimize $C = 0.23x_1 + 0.02x_2$
Subject to $13x_1 + 5x_2 \ge 44$
$19x_1 + 31x_2 \ge 55$
$x_1, x_2 \ge 0$

[8]   126 bottles of white wine, and 12 bottles of red wine

[9]   Maximum at (6, 4)

[10]  Maximum occurs at (12, 5) and is 85.

[11]
Basic variables: $x_1$, $s_2$
Nonbasic variables: $x_2$, $s_1$
Solution is feasible.

[12]
$x_1 = 12$, $x_2 = 5$
The basic solution is feasible.

[13]
$5x_1 + 8x_2 + s_1 \qquad\qquad = 25$
$9x_1 + 6x_2 \qquad + s_2 \qquad = 30$
$8x_1 - 9x_2 \qquad\qquad + s_3 \quad = 30$
$-25x_1 + 30x_2 \qquad\qquad\qquad + P = 0$
$x_1, x_2 \ge 0$
$s_1, s_2, s_3 \ge 0$

[14]  $x_1 = 36$, $x_2 = 0$, $x_3 = 0$, $s_1 = 15$, $s_2 = 6$, $s_3 = 0$, $P = 40$

[15]

Enter

|        |       | $x_1$ | $x_2$ | $s_1$ | $s_2$ | $s_3$ | $s_4$ | $P$ |     |
|--------|-------|-------|-------|-------|-------|-------|-------|-----|-----|
|        | $s_1$ | -1    | 7     | 1     | 0     | 0     | 0     | 0   | 4   |
|        | $s_2$ | 0     | 7     | 0     | 1     | 0     | 0     | 0   | 5   |
|        | $s_3$ | 5     | 8     | 0     | 0     | 1     | 0     | 0   | 9   |
| Exit   | $s_4$ | (5)   | 1     | 0     | 0     | 0     | 1     | 0   | 8   |
|        |       | -8    | -5    | 0     | 0     | 0     | 0     | 1   | 0   |

## Key Sheet - CHAPTER 6

[16]

$$\left[ \begin{array}{cccccc|c} 3 & -\frac{3}{4} & 0 & 0 & 1 & 0 & 3 \\ -1 & \frac{1}{4} & 1 & 0 & 0 & 0 & 2 \\ 7 & -1 & 0 & 1 & 0 & 0 & 8 \\ \hline -15 & 2 & 0 & 0 & 0 & 1 & 56 \end{array} \right]$$

[17] An additional pivot is required.

[18] Max $P = 1$ at $x_1 = 0$ and $x_2 = 1$

Essentials of College Mathematics, Third Edition
Raymond A. Barnett and Michael R. Ziegler

CHAPTER 6   Linear Inequalities and Linear Programming

1.   Graph: $7x - 6y \geq 42$

2.   Solve the following system graphically: $x \leq -1$
                                             $y > 2$
                                             $4x + 2y < 16$

3.   Find the coordinates of the corner points of the solution region for:
     $2x + 4y \geq 48$
     $x + 5y \leq 30$
     $x \geq 0$
     $y \geq 0$

4.   Formulate the following problem as a linear programming problem (DO
     NOT SOLVE):
     A small accounting firm prepares tax returns for two types of
     customers: individuals and small businesses.  Data is collected during
     an interview.  A computer system is used to produce the tax return.
     It takes 2 hours to enter data into the computer for an individual
     tax return and 4 hours to enter data for a small business tax
     return.  There is a maximum of 50 hours per week for data entry.  It
     takes 10 minutes for the computer to process an individual tax return
     and 15 minutes to process a small business tax return.  The computer
     is available for a maximum of 1,000 minutes per week.  The accounting
     firm makes a profit of $275 on each individual tax return processed
     and a profit of $300 on each small business tax return processed.
     How many of each type of tax return should the firm schedule each
     week in order to maximize its profit?  (Let $x_1$ equal the number of
     individual tax returns and $x_2$ the number of small business tax
     returns.)

5.   Formulate the following problem as a linear programming problem (DO
     NOT SOLVE):
     A company which produces three kinds of spaghetti sauce has two
     plants.  The East plant produces 3,500 jars of plain sauce, 2,500 jars
     of sauce with mushrooms, and 5,500 jars of hot spicy sauce per day.
     The West plant produces 6,000 jars of plain sauce, 4,500 jars of sauce
     with mushrooms, and 2,000 jars of hot spicy sauce per day.  The cost
     to operate the East plant is $8,000 per day and the cost to operate
     the West plant is $6,500 per day.  How many days should each plant
     operate to minimize cost and to fill an order for at least 6,000 jars
     of plain sauce, 6,500 jars of sauce with mushrooms, and 8,000 jars of
     hot spicy sauce?  (Let $x_1$ equal the number of days East plant should
     operate and $x_2$ the number of days West plant should operate.)

CHAPTER 6    Linear Inequalities and Linear Programming

6.    Formulate the following problem as a linear programming problem
      (DO NOT SOLVE):
      A steel company produces two types of machine dies, part A and
      part B.  Part A requires 5 hours of casting time and 2 hours of
      firing time.  Part B requires 6 hours of casting time and 9 hours
      of firing time.  The maximum number of hours per week available for
      casting and firing are 95 and 85, respectively.  The company makes
      a $9.00 profit on each part A that it produces, and a $2.00 profit
      on each part B that it produces.  How many of each type should the
      company produce each week in order to maximize its profit?  (Let
      $x_1$ equal the number of A parts and $x_2$ equal the number of B parts

      produced each week.)

7.    Formulate the following problem as a linear programming problem
      (DO NOT SOLVE):
      A dietician can purchase an ounce of chicken for $0.19 and an
      ounce of potatoes for $0.03.  Each ounce of chicken contains 18
      units of protein and 22 units of carbohydrates.  Each ounce of
      potatoes contains 9 units of protein and 23 units of
      carbohydrates.  The minimum daily requirements for the patients
      under the dietician's care are 44 units of protein and 64 units of
      carbohydrates.  How many ounces of each type of food should the
      dietician purchase for each patient so as to minimize costs and at
      the same time insure the minimum daily requirements of protein and
      carbohydrates?  (Let $x_1$ equal the number of ounces of chicken and $x_2$

      the number of ounces of potatoes purchased per patient.)

8.    A vineyard produces two special wines, a white, and a red.  A
      bottle of the white wine requires 3 pounds of grapes and 1 hour
      of processing time.  A bottle of the red wine requires 3 pounds
      of grapes and 2 hours of processing time.  The vineyard has on hand
      381 pounds of grapes and can allot 130 hours of processing time to
      the production of these wines.  A bottle of the white wine sells for
      $15.00, while a bottle of the red wine sells for $28.00.  How
      many bottles of each type should the vineyard produce in order to
      maximize gross sales?  (Solve using the geometric method.)

CHAPTER 6    Linear Inequalities and Linear Programming

9.    Solve the following linear programming problem by determining the
      feasible region on the graph below and testing the corner points:
      Maximize $P = x_1 + 6x_2$
      Subject to $4x_1 + 3x_2 \leq 36$
      $\phantom{Subject to} 2x_1 + x_2 \geq 14$
      $\phantom{Subject to xxx} x_1, x_2 \geq 0$

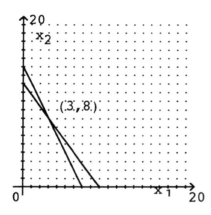

10.   The corner points for the bounded feasible region determined by the
      system of inequalities:
      $4x_1 + 2x_2 \leq 64$
      $3x_1 + 5x_2 \leq 90$
      $\phantom{3xx} x_1, x_2 \geq 0$
      are  $O = (0, 0)$, $A = (0, 18)$, $B = (10, 12)$ and $C = (16, 0)$.  Find the
      optimal solution for the objective profit function:
      $P = 4x_1 + 4x_2$

11.   A basic solution for the system:
      $x_1 + 3x_2 + s_1 \phantom{xxx} = 18$
      $2x_1 + 4x_2 \phantom{xxx} + s_2 = 32$
      is $x_1 = 0$, $x_2 = 8$, $s_1 = -6$, $s_2 = 0$.
      Identify the basic and nonbasic variables and determine if the
      solution is feasible or not feasible.

## CHAPTER 6    Linear Inequalities and Linear Programming

12. For the following linear system associated with a linear programming problem, find the value of the basic variables and determine if the basic solution is feasible:

    $x_1 + 5x_2 + s_1 \qquad = 35$

    $4x_1 + 3x_2 \qquad + s_2 = 72$

    if $x_1$ and $s_1$ are chosen as nonbasic variables.

13. Using slack variables, write the initial system for the following linear programming problem:

    Maximize $P = 30x_1 - 20x_2$

    Subject to $4x_1 + 9x_2 \leq 15$

    $\qquad\qquad 2x_1 + 5x_2 \leq 15$

    $\qquad\qquad 9x_1 - 2x_2 \leq 20$

    $\qquad\qquad\qquad x_1, \; x_2 \geq 0$

14. Write the basic solution for the following simplex tableau:

$$
\begin{array}{ccccccc}
x_1 & x_2 & x_3 & s_1 & s_2 & s_3 & P \\
\end{array}
$$

$$
\left[
\begin{array}{ccccccc|c}
1 & -3 & 9 & 0 & 0 & 1 & 0 & 12 \\
0 & 10 & 3 & 0 & 1 & 1 & 0 & 18 \\
0 & 0 & 10 & 1 & 0 & 0 & 0 & 30 \\
\hline
0 & -4 & -9 & 0 & 0 & 4 & 1 & 35
\end{array}
\right]
$$

15. Write the simplex tableau, label the columns and rows, circle the pivot element, and identify the entering and exiting variables for the linear programming problem:

    Maximize $P = 5x_1 + 2x_2$

    Subject to $\qquad\qquad 7x_2 \leq 2$

    $\qquad\qquad -3x_1 + 7x_2 \leq 12$

    $\qquad\qquad\quad 2x_1 + 5x_2 \leq 6$

    $\qquad\qquad\quad 2x_1 + 3x_2 \leq 5$

    $\qquad\qquad\qquad\quad x_1, \; x_2 \geq 0$

16. Perform the next pivot operation on the following simplex tableau and write the resulting tableau:

$$
\left[
\begin{array}{cccccc|c}
0 & 0 & 5 & 0 & 1 & 0 & 15 \\
5 & 0 & 2 & 1 & 0 & 0 & 8 \\
-2 & 1 & 2 & 0 & 0 & 0 & 4 \\
\hline
-5 & 0 & -6 & 0 & 0 & 1 & 35
\end{array}
\right]
$$

CHAPTER 6    Linear Inequalities and Linear Programming

17.  State whether the optimal solution has been found, an additional
     pivot is required, or there is no solution for the problem
     corresponding to the following simplex tableau:

$$
\begin{array}{ccccccc}
x_1 & x_2 & x_3 & s_1 & s_2 & s_3 & P \\
\end{array}
$$

$$
\left[
\begin{array}{ccccccc|c}
-2 & 0 & 0 & 3 & 1 & 1 & 0 & 8 \\
-4 & 0 & 1 & 2 & 1 & 0 & 0 & 5 \\
0 & 1 & 0 & -2 & 0 & 0 & 0 & 40 \\
\hline
-1 & 0 & 0 & 5 & 2 & 0 & 1 & 51 \\
\end{array}
\right]
$$

18.  Solve the following linear programming problem using the simplex
     method:

Maximize $P = x_1 - x_2$

Subject to  $x_1 + x_2 \leq 4$

$2x_1 + 7x_2 \leq 14$

$x_1, x_2 \geq 0$

Key Sheet - CHAPTER 6

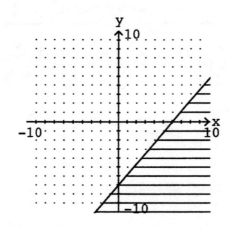

[1] _____

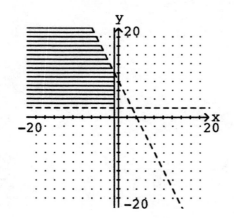

[2] _____

[3]  (24, 0), (30, 0), (20, 2)
     _____

     Maximize P = $275x_1 + 300x_2$
     Subject to $2x_1 + 4x_2 \leq 50$
                $10x_1 + 15x_2 \leq 1,000$
[4]              $x_1,\ x_2 \geq 0$
     _____

     Minimize C = $8,000x_1 + 6,500x_2$
     Subject to $3,500x_1 + 6,000x_2 \geq 6,000$
                $2,500x_1 + 4,500x_2 \geq 6,500$
                $5,500x_1 + 2,000x_2 \geq 8,000$
[5]              $x_1,\ x_2 \geq 0$
     _____

Key Sheet - CHAPTER 6

[6]
Maximize $P = 9x_1 + 2x_2$
Subject to $5x_1 + 6x_2 \leq 95$
$\phantom{Subject to }2x_1 + 9x_2 \leq 85$
$\phantom{Subject to }x_1,\ x_2 \geq 0$

[7]
Minimize $C = 0.19x_1 + 0.03x_2$
Subject to $18x_1 + 9x_2 \geq 44$
$\phantom{Subject to }22x_1 + 23x_2 \geq 64$
$\phantom{Subject to }x_1,\ x_2 \geq 0$

[8] 124 bottles of white wine, and 3 bottles of red wine

[9] Maximum at (3, 8)

[10] Maximum occurs at (10, 12) and is 88.

[11]
Basic variables: $x_2$, $s_1$
Nonbasic variables: $x_1$, $s_2$
Solution is not feasible.

[12]
$x_2 = 7$, $s_2 = 51$
The basic solution is feasible.

[13]
$$4x_1 + 9x_2 + s_1 \phantom{+ s_2 + s_3 + P} = 15$$
$$2x_1 + 5x_2 \phantom{+ s_1} + s_2 \phantom{+ s_3 + P} = 15$$
$$9x_1 - 2x_2 \phantom{+ s_1 + s_2} + s_3 \phantom{+ P} = 20$$
$$-30x_1 + 20x_2 \phantom{+ s_1 + s_2 + s_3} + P = 0$$
$$x_1,\ x_2 \geq 0$$
$$s_1,\ s_2,\ s_3 \geq 0$$

[14] $x_1 = 12$, $x_2 = 0$, $x_3 = 0$, $s_1 = 30$, $s_2 = 18$, $s_3 = 0$, $P = 35$

[15]

|  |  | Enter |  |  |  |  |  |  |  |
|  |  | $x_1$ | $x_2$ | $s_1$ | $s_2$ | $s_3$ | $s_4$ | $P$ |  |
|  | $s_1$ | 0 | 7 | 1 | 0 | 0 | 0 | 0 | 2 |
|  | $s_2$ | -3 | 7 | 0 | 1 | 0 | 0 | 0 | 12 |
|  | $s_3$ | 2 | 5 | 0 | 0 | 1 | 0 | 0 | 6 |
| Exit | $s_4$ | (2) | 3 | 0 | 0 | 0 | 1 | 0 | 5 |
|  |  | -5 | -2 | 0 | 0 | 0 | 0 | 1 | 0 |

## Key Sheet - CHAPTER 6

[16]
$$\left[\begin{array}{cccccc|c} 5 & -\dfrac{5}{2} & 0 & 0 & 1 & 0 & 5 \\ 7 & -1 & 0 & 1 & 0 & 0 & 4 \\ -1 & \dfrac{1}{2} & 1 & 0 & 0 & 0 & 2 \\ \hline -11 & 3 & 0 & 0 & 0 & 1 & 47 \end{array}\right]$$

[17] There is no solution.

[18] Max $P = 4$ at $x_1 = 4$ and $x_2 = 0$

Essentials of College Mathematics, Third Edition
Raymond A. Barnett and Michael R. Ziegler

CHAPTER 7    Probability

1.   A coin that can turn up either heads (H) or tails (T) is flipped.  If
     a head turns up, a spinner that can land on any of the first 5 natural
     numbers is spun.  If a tail turns up, the coin is flipped a second
     time.  What are the different possible outcomes?

2.   A person purchasing a new car has several options: 3 interior color
     choices, 3 exterior color choices, 2 choices of radios, and 3 choices
     of body styles.  How many different cars are possible if one choice
     is made for each option?

3.   A test is composed of 5 multiple choice problems and 10 questions
     that can be answered true or false.  Each multiple choice problem has
     4 choices.  How many different response sheets are possible if only
     one choice is marked for each question?

4.   How many five-digit ZIP code numbers are possible if the first digit
     cannot be a four and adjacent digits cannot be the same?

5.   A combination lock on a suitcase has 5 wheels, each labeled with
     digits 1 to 8.  How many 5-digit combination lock codes are possible
     if no digit can be repeated?

6.   A survey of residents in a certain town indicates 90 own a
     dehumidifier, 100 own a microwave oven, and 60 own a dehumidifier
     and a microwave oven.  How many own a dehumidifier or a
     microwave oven?

7.   In a group of 275 people, 155 invest in mutual funds, 165 invest in
     stocks, and 70 invest in mutual funds and stocks.  How
     many people in this group invest in neither mutual funds nor
     stocks?

8.   From a group of 6 people, in how many ways can we choose a
     chairperson, vice-chairperson, treasurer, and secretary, assuming one
     person cannot hold more than one position?

9.   A company is to choose 6 persons from the sales department to go to
     a convention in the Bahamas.  There are 12 people in the sales
     department.  In how many ways can this group of 6 be chosen?

10.  How many ways can a committee of 3 Democrats and 2 Republicans be
     selected from a state legislature that contains 9 Democrats and
     11 Republicans?

11.  A software company employs 7 sales representatives and 9 technical
     representatives.  How many ways can the company select 3 of these
     employees to send to a computer convention if at least 2 sales
     representatives must attend the convention?

CHAPTER 7    Probability

12.  A spinner that has 5 sections of equal area, numbered from 1 to 5, is spun two times in succession.  Find the sample space composed of equally likely events.

13.  An experiment consists of drawing a ball from a box which contains nine balls numbered 1 to 9.  The sample space of equally likely simple events is {1, 2, 3, 4, 5, 6, 7, 8, 9}.  What is the probability of the event associated with the outcome being a prime number?

14.  A box contains 9 red, 6 white, 7 black, and 8 yellow marbles.  If we choose a sample space for a single draw to be S = {R, W, B, Y}, which of the following probability assignments is the most suitable?

   A)   $P(R) = \frac{1}{4}$, $P(W) = \frac{1}{4}$, $P(B) = \frac{1}{4}$, $P(Y) = \frac{1}{4}$

   B)   $P(R) = 1$, $P(W) = 0$, $P(B) = \frac{7}{30}$, $P(Y) = \frac{8}{30}$

   C)   $P(R) = \frac{1}{9}$, $P(W) = \frac{1}{6}$, $P(B) = \frac{1}{7}$, $P(Y) = \frac{1}{8}$

   D)   $P(R) = \frac{9}{30}$, $P(W) = \frac{6}{30}$, $P(B) = \frac{7}{30}$, $P(Y) = \frac{8}{30}$

15.  An urn contains 7 dimes and 3 quarters.  Two coins are removed from the urn, one after the other, without replacement, and the total value of the two coins is recorded.  Find an appropriate sample space for this experiment and find the probability of each simple event in the sample space.

16.  A committee of 6 people is to be chosen from a group of 5 men and 7 women.  What is the probability that the committee will consist of 4 men and 2 women?

17.  A department store receives a shipment of 25 new portable radios.  There are 3 defective radios in the shipment.  If 5 radios are selected for display, what is the probability that 2 of them are defective?

18.  Ten cards are drawn from a standard deck of cards.  What is the probability that there are 3 face cards and 7 non-face cards?

## CHAPTER 7    Probability

19. A poll was conducted preceding an election to determine the relationship between voter persuasion concerning a controversial issue and the area of the city in which the voter lives. Five hundred registered voters were interviewed from three areas of the city. The data are shown below. Compute the probability of having no opinion on the issue or living in the inner city.

|              | Voter opinion | | |
| Area of city | Favor | Oppose | No Opinion |
| --- | --- | --- | --- |
| East  | 60 | 45 | 40 |
| North | 25 | 55 | 65 |
| Inner | 95 | 70 | 45 |

20. A group of 40 people was classified according to sex and age. Find the probability of a person chosen at random from this group being a male less than age 20.

|        | Age | |
| Sex    | 20 or older | Less than 20 |
| --- | --- | --- |
| Male   | 6 | 22 |
| Female | 9 | 3 |

21. A survey of men and women pet owners found that 30 owned a dog, 30 owned a cat, 4 owned a bird, and 1 owned a gerbil. Of the women, 20 owned a dog, 20 owned a cat, 3 owned a bird, and 0 owned a gerbil. No person owned more than one pet. What is the probability that a person chosen at random from this group is male and owned a cat or a dog?

22. The probability distribution for the random variable X is:

| $x_i$ | -1 | 0 | 1 | 2 |
| --- | --- | --- | --- | --- |
| $p_i$ | 0.22 | 0.16 | 0.18 | 0.44 |

What is the expected value of X?

23. Volunteers for a charity raffle sold 1,000 tickets at $15 each. Tickets are to be drawn at random and monetary prizes are awarded as follows: one prize of $600; two prizes of $500; five prizes of $300; and ten prizes of $100. What is the expected value of this raffle to you if you buy one ticket?

## CHAPTER 7    Probability

24. A $3,000 stereo system is insured against need of repair in the first year for an annual premium of $15. The probability of repair in the first year is .10, and the average cost of repair in the first year is $60. What is the expected value of the policy to the owner of the stereo if insurance is purchased?

25. A quality control engineer selects a random sample of 3 disk drives, from a group of 34 coming off an assembly line, to test for defects. Let X be the random variable associated with the number of defects in the sample. If there are 4 defective disk drives in the group of 34, find the expected value of the random variable X.

26. An art dealer plans to send a large sculpture collection on a national tour. If the entire collection completes the tour, the dealer will earn a net profit of $80,000 from admissions proceeds. If some of the pieces are damaged in shipping and handling, they will have to be returned, and the diminished collection will earn a net profit of only $9,000. There is a probability of 0.25 that such damage will occur. An insurance company is willing to insure the tour for $80,000 in case of such damage, for a premium of $20,000. What is the expected net profit if the art dealer buys the insurance? If the art dealer does not buy insurance?

27. The payoff table for three possible courses of action $A_1$, $A_2$ and $A_3$ is given below.

| $p_i$ | $A_1$ $x_i$ | $A_2$ $x_i$ | $A_3$ $x_i$ |
|---|---|---|---|
| 0.2 | $ 70 | $ 50 | $ 40 |
| 0.4 | $100 | $120 | $110 |
| 0.1 | $140 | $160 | $ 90 |
| 0.3 | $ 80 | $ 90 | $140 |

Which course of action will produce the largest expected value? What is it?

## Key Sheet - CHAPTER 7

[1] {(H, 1), (H, 2), (H, 3), (H, 4), (H, 5), (T, H), (T, T)}

[2] (3)(3)(3)(2) = 54

[3] $(4^5)(2^{10})$ = 1,048,576

[4] $9^5$ = 59,049

[5] 6,720

[6] 130

[7] 25

[8] 360

[9] 924

[10] 4,620

[11] 224

[12] {(1, 1), (1, 2), (1, 3), (1, 4), (1, 5),
(2, 1), (2, 2), (2, 3), (2, 4), (2, 5),
(3, 1), (3, 2), (3, 3), (3, 4), (3, 5),
(4, 1), (4, 2), (4, 3), (4, 4), (4, 5),
(5, 1), (5, 2), (5, 3), (5, 4), (5, 5)}

[13] $\frac{4}{9} \approx 0.444$

[14] D

[15]

| $x_i$ | $0.20 | $0.35 | $0.50 |
|-------|-------|-------|-------|
| $P_i$ | 0.467 | 0.467 | 0.067 |

[16] $\frac{5}{44} \approx 0.114$

[17] 0.087

[18] 0.26

[19] $\frac{315}{500}$ = 0.630

## Key Sheet - CHAPTER 7

[20] $\frac{22}{40}$ = 0.550

[21] $\frac{20}{65}$ ≈ 0.308

[22] 0.84

[23] -$10.90

[24] -$9.00

[25] $E(X)$ = 0.35

[26] If insured $E(X)$ = 62,250, if not insured $E(X)$ = 62,250, therefore dealer should not buy insurance.

[27] $A_3$ has the largest expected value.
$E(A_3)$ = 103

## CHAPTER 7   Probability

1.  A coin that can turn up either heads (H) or tails (T) is flipped.  If a head turns up, a spinner that can land on any of the first 4 natural numbers is spun.  If a tail turns up, the coin is flipped a second time.  What are the different possible outcomes?

2.  A person purchasing a new car has several options: 4 interior color choices, 3 exterior color choices, 2 choices of radios, and 5 choices of body styles.  How many different cars are possible if one choice is made for each option?

3.  A test is composed of 4 multiple choice problems and 7 questions that can be answered true or false.  Each multiple choice problem has 5 choices.  How many different response sheets are possible if only one choice is marked for each question?

4.  How many nine-digit ZIP code numbers are possible if the first digit cannot be a two and adjacent digits cannot be the same?

5.  A combination lock on a suitcase has 4 wheels, each labeled with digits 1 to 8.  How many 4-digit combination lock codes are possible if no digit can be repeated?

6.  A survey of residents in a certain town indicates 140 own a snow blower, 110 own a lawn mower, and 40 own a snow blower and a lawn mower.  How many own a snow blower or a lawn mower?

7.  In a group of 285 people, 155 invest in mutual funds, 140 invest in money markets, and 60 invest in mutual funds and money markets.  How many people in this group invest in neither mutual funds nor money markets?

8.  From a group of 10 people, in how many ways can we choose a chairperson, vice-chairperson, treasurer, and secretary, assuming one person cannot hold more than one position?

9.  A company is to choose 3 persons from the sales department to go to a convention in the Bahamas.  There are 8 people in the sales department.  In how many ways can this group of 3 be chosen?

10. How many ways can a committee of 5 Democrats and 3 Republicans be selected from a state legislature that contains 8 Democrats and 11 Republicans?

11. A software company employs 8 sales representatives and 10 technical representatives.  How many ways can the company select 3 of these employees to send to a computer convention if at least 2 sales representatives must attend the convention?

CHAPTER 7    Probability

12.  A spinner that has 3 sections of equal area, numbered from 1 to 3, is spun two times in succession.  Find the sample space composed of equally likely events.

13.  An experiment consists of drawing a ball from a box which contains nine balls numbered 1 to 9.  The sample space of equally likely simple events is {1, 2, 3, 4, 5, 6, 7, 8, 9}.  What is the probability of the event associated with the outcome being an odd number?

14.  A box contains 6 red, 3 white, 5 black, and 8 yellow marbles.  If we choose a sample space for a single draw to be S = {R, W, B, Y}, which of the following probability assignments is the most suitable?

A)   $P(R) = \frac{6}{22}$, $P(W) = \frac{3}{22}$, $P(B) = \frac{5}{22}$, $P(Y) = \frac{8}{22}$

B)   $P(R) = \frac{1}{6}$, $P(W) = \frac{1}{3}$, $P(B) = \frac{1}{5}$, $P(Y) = \frac{1}{8}$

C)   $P(R) = \frac{1}{4}$, $P(W) = \frac{1}{4}$, $P(B) = \frac{1}{4}$, $P(Y) = \frac{1}{4}$

D)   $P(R) = 1$, $P(W) = 0$, $P(B) = \frac{5}{22}$, $P(Y) = \frac{8}{22}$

15.  An urn contains 5 dimes and 10 quarters.  Two coins are removed from the urn, one after the other, without replacement, and the total value of the two coins is recorded.  Find an appropriate sample space for this experiment and find the probability of each simple event in the sample space.

16.  A committee of 6 people is to be chosen from a group of 7 men and 5 women.  What is the probability that the committee will consist of 4 men and 2 women?

17.  A department store receives a shipment of 22 new portable radios.  There are 4 defective radios in the shipment.  If 7 radios are selected for display, what is the probability that 2 of them are defective?

18.  Eight cards are drawn from a standard deck of cards.  What is the probability that there are 6 face cards and 2 non-face cards?

CHAPTER 7    Probability

19. A poll was conducted preceding an election to determine the relationship between voter persuasion concerning a controversial issue and the area of the city in which the voter lives. Five hundred registered voters were interviewed from three areas of the city. The data are shown below. Compute the probability of having no opinion on the issue or living in the inner city.

| | Voter opinion | | |
| Area of city | Favor | Oppose | No Opinion |
| --- | --- | --- | --- |
| East | 60 | 45 | 40 |
| North | 25 | 55 | 65 |
| Inner | 75 | 60 | 75 |

20. A group of 40 people was classified according to sex and age. Find the probability of a person chosen at random from this group being a male less than age 20.

| | Age | |
| Sex | 20 or older | Less than 20 |
| --- | --- | --- |
| Male | 3 | 16 |
| Female | 17 | 4 |

21. A survey of men and women pet owners found that 25 owned a dog, 25 owned a cat, 4 owned a bird, and 3 owned a gerbil. Of the women, 10 owned a dog, 15 owned a cat, 4 owned a bird, and 2 owned a gerbil. No person owned more than one pet. What is the probability that a person chosen at random from this group is male and owned a cat or a dog?

22. The probability distribution for the random variable X is:

| $x_i$ | -1 | 0 | 1 | 2 |
| --- | --- | --- | --- | --- |
| $p_i$ | 0.19 | 0.20 | 0.25 | 0.36 |

What is the expected value of X?

23. Volunteers for a charity raffle sold 500 tickets at $10 each. Tickets are to be drawn at random and monetary prizes are awarded as follows: one prize of $800; two prizes of $450; five prizes of $200; and ten prizes of $50. What is the expected value of this raffle to you if you buy one ticket?

CHAPTER 7    Probability

24.  A $2,500 stereo system is insured against need of repair in the first
     year for an annual premium of $10.  The probability of repair in the
     first year is .30, and the average cost of repair in the first year
     is $50.  What is the expected value of the policy to the owner of the
     stereo if insurance is purchased?

25.  A quality control engineer selects a random sample of 3 disk drives,
     from a group of 27 coming off an assembly line, to test for defects.
     Let X be the random variable associated with the number of defects in
     the sample.  If there are 4 defective disk drives in the group
     of 27, find the expected value of the random variable X.

26.  An art dealer plans to send a large sculpture collection on a national
     tour.  If the entire collection completes the tour, the dealer will
     earn a net profit of $80,000 from admissions proceeds.  If some of the
     pieces are damaged in shipping and handling, they will have to be
     returned, and the diminished collection will earn a net profit of only
     $12,000.  There is a probability of 0.15 that such damage will occur.
     An insurance company is willing to insure the tour for $80,000 in case
     of such damage, for a premium of $20,000.  What is the expected net
     profit if the art dealer buys the insurance?  If the art dealer does
     not buy insurance?

27.  The payoff table for three possible courses of action $A_1$,
     $A_2$ and $A_3$ is given below.

| $p_i$ | $A_1$ $x_i$ | $A_2$ $x_i$ | $A_3$ $x_i$ |
|-------|-------------|-------------|-------------|
| 0.3   | $ 70        | $ 50        | $ 40        |
| 0.4   | $110        | $120        | $100        |
| 0.1   | $160        | $ 90        | $140        |
| 0.2   | $110        | $140        | $ 90        |

Which course of action will produce the largest expected
value?  What is it?

## Key Sheet - CHAPTER 7

[1] $\{(H, 1), (H, 2), (H, 3), (H, 4),$ $(T, H), (T, T)\}$

[2] $(4)(3)(5)(2) = 120$

[3] $(5^4)(2^7) = 80,000$

[4] $9^9 = 387,420,489$

[5] 1,680

[6] 210

[7] 50

[8] 5,040

[9] 56

[10] 9,240

[11] 336

[12] $\{(1, 1), (1, 2), (1, 3),$ $(2, 1), (2, 2), (2, 3),$ $(3, 1), (3, 2), (3, 3)\}$

[13] $\frac{5}{9} \approx 0.556$

[14] A

[15]

| $x_i$ | \$0.20 | \$0.35 | \$0.50 |
|-------|--------|--------|--------|
| $P_i$ | 0.095 | 0.476 | 0.429 |

[16] $\frac{25}{66} \approx 0.379$

[17] 0.30

[18] 0.00096

[19] $\frac{315}{500} = 0.630$

[20] $\frac{16}{40} = 0.400$

## Key Sheet – CHAPTER 7

[21] $\frac{25}{57} \approx 0.439$

[22] 0.78

[23] –$3.60

[24] $5.00

[25] $E(X) = 0.44$

[26] If insured $E(X) = 61,800$, if not insured $E(X) = 69,800$, therefore dealer should not buy insurance.

[27] $A_1$ has the largest expected value.
$E(A_1) = 103$

Essentials of College Mathematics, Third Edition
Raymond A. Barnett and Michael R. Ziegler

CHAPTER 7    Probability

1.    A coin that can turn up either heads (H) or tails (T) is flipped.  If
      a head turns up, a spinner that can land on any of the first 6 natural
      numbers is spun.  If a tail turns up, the coin is flipped a second
      time.  What are the different possible outcomes?

2.    A person purchasing a new car has several options: 5 interior color
      choices, 6 exterior color choices, 2 choices of radios, and 6 choices
      of body styles.  How many different cars are possible if one choice
      is made for each option?

3.    A test is composed of 7 multiple choice problems and 8 questions
      that can be answered true or false.  Each multiple choice problem has
      3 choices.  How many different response sheets are possible if only
      one choice is marked for each question?

4.    How many five-digit ZIP code numbers are possible if the first digit
      cannot be a two and adjacent digits cannot be the same?

5.    A combination lock on a suitcase has 3 wheels, each labeled with
      digits 1 to 8.  How many 3-digit combination lock codes are possible
      if no digit can be repeated?

6.    A survey of residents in a certain town indicates 70 own a
      dishwasher, 150 own a lawn mower, and 50 own a dishwasher
      and a lawn mower.  How many own a dishwasher or a
      lawn mower?

7.    In a group of 260 people, 160 invest in mutual funds, 140 invest in
      bonds, and 75 invest in mutual funds and bonds.  How
      many people in this group invest in neither mutual funds nor
      bonds?

8.    From a group of 8 people, in how many ways can we choose a
      chairperson, vice-chairperson, treasurer, and secretary, assuming one
      person cannot hold more than one position?

9.    A company is to choose 4 persons from the sales department to go to
      a convention in the Bahamas.  There are 9 people in the sales
      department.  In how many ways can this group of 4 be chosen?

10.   How many ways can a committee of 4 Democrats and 5 Republicans be
      selected from a state legislature that contains 9 Democrats and
      11 Republicans?

11.   A software company employs 9 sales representatives and 7 technical
      representatives.  How many ways can the company select 4 of these
      employees to send to a computer convention if at least 3 sales
      representatives must attend the convention?

---

CHAPTER 7    Probability

---

12.  A spinner that has 4 sections of equal area, numbered from 1 to 4, is spun two times in succession. Find the sample space composed of equally likely events.

13.  An experiment consists of drawing a ball from a box which contains nine balls numbered 1 to 9. The sample space of equally likely simple events is {1, 2, 3, 4, 5, 6, 7, 8, 9}. What is the probability of the event associated with the outcome being divisible by three?

14.  A box contains 7 red, 9 white, 4 black, and 6 yellow marbles. If we choose a sample space for a single draw to be S = {R, W, B, Y}, which of the following probability assignments is the most suitable?

   A)   $P(R) = 1$, $P(W) = 0$, $P(B) = \frac{4}{26}$, $P(Y) = \frac{6}{26}$

   B)   $P(R) = \frac{1}{4}$, $P(W) = \frac{1}{4}$, $P(B) = \frac{1}{4}$, $P(Y) = \frac{1}{4}$

   C)   $P(R) = \frac{1}{7}$, $P(W) = \frac{1}{9}$, $P(B) = \frac{1}{4}$, $P(Y) = \frac{1}{6}$

   D)   $P(R) = \frac{7}{26}$, $P(W) = \frac{9}{26}$, $P(B) = \frac{4}{26}$, $P(Y) = \frac{6}{26}$

15.  An urn contains 3 dimes and 7 quarters. Two coins are removed from the urn, one after the other, without replacement, and the total value of the two coins is recorded. Find an appropriate sample space for this experiment and find the probability of each simple event in the sample space.

16.  A committee of 4 people is to be chosen from a group of 6 men and 5 women. What is the probability that the committee will consist of 2 men and 2 women?

17.  A department store receives a shipment of 28 new portable radios. There are 5 defective radios in the shipment. If 6 radios are selected for display, what is the probability that 2 of them are defective?

18.  Nine cards are drawn from a standard deck of cards. What is the probability that there are 2 face cards and 7 non-face cards?

CHAPTER 7    Probability

19. A poll was conducted preceding an election to determine the relationship between voter persuasion concerning a controversial issue and the area of the city in which the voter lives. Five hundred registered voters were interviewed from three areas of the city. The data are shown below. Compute the probability of having no opinion on the issue or living in the inner city.

| Area of city | Voter opinion | | |
| | Favor | Oppose | No Opinion |
|---|---|---|---|
| East | 60 | 45 | 40 |
| North | 25 | 55 | 65 |
| Inner | 95 | 70 | 45 |

20. A group of 40 people was classified according to sex and age. Find the probability of a person chosen at random from this group being a male less than age 20.

| Sex | Age | |
| | 20 or older | Less than 20 |
|---|---|---|
| Male | 5 | 24 |
| Female | 5 | 6 |

21. A survey of men and women pet owners found that 35 owned a dog, 25 owned a cat, 4 owned a bird, and 1 owned a gerbil. Of the women, 15 owned a dog, 10 owned a cat, 3 owned a bird, and 1 owned a gerbil. No person owned more than one pet. What is the probability that a person chosen at random from this group is male and owned a cat or a dog?

22. The probability distribution for the random variable X is:

| $x_i$ | -1 | 0 | 1 | 2 |
|---|---|---|---|---|
| $p_i$ | 0.16 | 0.20 | 0.17 | 0.47 |

What is the expected value of X?

23. Volunteers for a charity raffle sold 500 tickets at $15 each. Tickets are to be drawn at random and monetary prizes are awarded as follows: one prize of $600; two prizes of $550; five prizes of $300; and ten prizes of $75. What is the expected value of this raffle to you if you buy one ticket?

CHAPTER 7    Probability

24. A $2,000 stereo system is insured against need of repair in the first year for an annual premium of $15. The probability of repair in the first year is .10, and the average cost of repair in the first year is $40. What is the expected value of the policy to the owner of the stereo if insurance is purchased?

25. A quality control engineer selects a random sample of 3 disk drives, from a group of 33 coming off an assembly line, to test for defects. Let X be the random variable associated with the number of defects in the sample. If there are 3 defective disk drives in the group of 33, find the expected value of the random variable X.

26. An art dealer plans to send a large sculpture collection on a national tour. If the entire collection completes the tour, the dealer will earn a net profit of $80,000 from admissions proceeds. If some of the pieces are damaged in shipping and handling, they will have to be returned, and the diminished collection will earn a net profit of only $6,000. There is a probability of 0.30 that such damage will occur. An insurance company is willing to insure the tour for $70,000 in case of such damage, for a premium of $20,000. What is the expected net profit if the art dealer buys the insurance? If the art dealer does not buy insurance?

27. The payoff table for three possible courses of action $A_1$, $A_2$ and $A_3$ is given below.

| $P_i$ | $A_1$ $x_i$ | $A_2$ $x_i$ | $A_3$ $x_i$ |
|---|---|---|---|
| 0.1 | $ 50 | $ 40 | $ 70 |
| 0.4 | $110 | $100 | $120 |
| 0.2 | $160 | $140 | $ 90 |
| 0.3 | $100 | $160 | $140 |

Which course of action will produce the largest expected value? What is it?

## Key Sheet – CHAPTER 7

[1]  $\{(H, 1), (H, 2), (H, 3), (H, 4), (H, 5), (H, 6),$
     $(T, H), (T, T)\}$

[2]  $(5)(6)(6)(2) = 360$

[3]  $(3^7)(2^8) = 559,872$

[4]  $9^5 = 59,049$

[5]  336

[6]  170

[7]  35

[8]  1,680

[9]  126

[10]  58,212

[11]  714

[12]  $\{(1, 1), (1, 2), (1, 3), (1, 4),$
      $(2, 1), (2, 2), (2, 3), (2, 4),$
      $(3, 1), (3, 2), (3, 3), (3, 4),$
      $(4, 1), (4, 2), (4, 3), (4, 4)\}$

[13]  $\frac{3}{9} \approx 0.333$

[14]  D

[15]

| $x_i$ | \$0.20 | \$0.35 | \$0.50 |
|-------|--------|--------|--------|
| $P_i$ | 0.067  | 0.467  | 0.467  |

[16]  $\frac{5}{11} \approx 0.455$

[17]  0.24

[18]  0.33

[19]  $\frac{315}{500} = 0.630$

[20] $\dfrac{24}{40} = 0.600$

[21] $\dfrac{35}{65} \approx 0.538$

[22] 0.95

[23] –$7.10

[24] –$11.00

[25] $E(X) = 0.27$

[26] If insured $E(X) = 58,800$, if not insured $E(X) = 57,800$, therefore dealer should buy insurance.

[27] $A_2$ has the largest expected value.
$E(A_2) = 120$

## CHAPTER 8    Additional Topics in Probability

1.  A spinner is numbered from 1 through 8 with each number as likely to occur as any other.  Compute the probability that in a single spin the dial will stop at a number less than 5 or greater than 7.

2.  A box contains pieces of paper numbered 2 through 8.  An appropriate sample space is S = {2, 3, 4,..., 8}.  A single piece of paper is to be drawn.  Let event A = {2, 4, 6, 8} and let event B = {2, 3, 4, 5}. What is the event A' ∩ B' ?

3.  A survey of 100 students at a large university found that 80 students played tennis, 45 played basketball, and 35 played both tennis and basketball.  If a student is selected at random, what is the (empirical) probability that the student plays tennis but not basketball?

4.  A group of 8 people consists of 2 men and 6 women.  A committee of 4 is chosen from this group.  What is the probability that one or more of the committee members is a man?

5.  A shipment of 29 compact disc players contains 5 that are defective.  If 7 players from this shipment are selected at random and tested, what is the probability that at least one defective player will be found?

6.  Three cards are randomly selected from a standard 52-card deck.  What is the probability of getting 3 hearts or 3 numbers less than 7 (count aces as 1)?

7.  A spinner is numbered from 1 through 7 with each number as likely to occur as any other.  On a single spin what are the odds in favor of the pointer landing on an even number or a number divisible by 3?

8.  The odds in favor of event A are 5:4.  What is the probability of A' ?

9.  Two groups of people were asked their preference in television programs from among three new programs.  The results are shown in the table below.  What is the probability that a person selected at random will be from group A or prefer program X?

| Group of People | Television Program | | |
|---|---|---|---|
|  | X | Y | Z |
| A | 20 | 40 | 25 |
| B | 45 | 15 | 55 |

CHAPTER 8    Additional Topics in Probability

10.  From a survey involving 2,000 students at a large university, it
     was found that 1,200 students had classes on Monday, Wednesday, and
     Friday; 1,300 students had classes on Tuesday and Thursday; and 500
     students had classes every day.  If a student at this university
     is selected at random, what is the (empirical) probability that
     the student has classes only on Tuesday and Thursday?

11.  A class of 50 students has 13 honor students and 12 athletes.  Three
     of the honor students are also athletes.  One student is chosen at
     random.  Find the probability that this student is an athlete if it
     is known that the student is not an honor student.

12.  A group of 25 people contains 10 brunettes, 8 blondes, and 7 redheads.
     Of the 20 girls in the group, 6 are brunettes, 8 are blondes, and 6
     are redheads.  A person is selected at random.  Are the events of
     being a girl and having brunette hair independent?

13.  A box contains 3 red balls and 6 white balls.  Two balls are to be
     drawn in succession without replacement.  What is the probability
     that the sample will contain exactly one white ball and one red ball?

14.  Suppose S is a sample space containing 160 equally likely simple
     events.  Assume A and B are events in this sample space with the
     following properties: there are 40 simple events in $A \cap B$; there
     are 40 simple events in A that are not in B; and there are 45
     simple events in B that are not in A.  Show why the events A and B
     are, or are not, independent.

15.  Refer to the tree diagram below to find P(A and B').

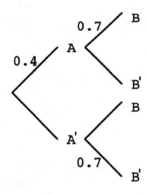

CHAPTER 8    Additional Topics in Probability

16. Each person in a group of students was identified by his or her hair color and then asked whether he or she preferred taking classes in the morning, afternoon, or evening. The results are shown in the table below. Find the probability that a student preferred morning classes given he or she has blonde hair.

| Class Time Preference | Hair Color | | |
|---|---|---|---|
|  | Blonde | Brunette | Redhead |
| Morning | 15 | 40 | 50 |
| Afternoon | 30 | 10 | 35 |
| Evening | 45 | 25 | 5 |

17. In building the space shuttle, NASA contracts for certain guidance components to be supplied by three different companies: 40% by company A, 42% by company B, and 18% by company C. It has been found that 1%, 1.75%, and 1.25% of the components from companies A, B, and C, respectively, are defective. If one of these guidance components is selected at random, what is the probability that it is defective?

18. One urn has 7 red balls and 2 white balls; a second urn has 2 red balls and 6 white balls. A single card is randomly selected from a standard deck. If the card is less than 9 (aces count as 1), a ball is drawn out of the first urn; otherwise a ball is drawn out of the second urn. If the drawn ball is red, what is the probability that it came out of the second urn?

19. A small manufacturing company has rated 85% of its employees as satisfactory (S) and 15% as unsatisfactory (S'). Personnel records show that 80% of the satisfactory workers had previous work experience (E) in the job they are now doing, while 25% of the unsatisfactory workers had no work experience (E') in the job they are now doing. If a person who has had no previous work experience is hired, what is the approximate empirical probability that this person will be a satisfactory employee?

20. A basketball team is to play two games in a tournament. The probability of winning the first game is 0.20. If the first game is won, the probability of winning the second game is 0.25. If the first game is lost, the probability of winning the second game is 0.10. What is the probability the first game was won if the second game is lost?

CHAPTER 8    Additional Topics in Probability

21.   Due to the continuous growth in the number of cases of measles
      reported from several different locations around the country, a drug
      company has developed a new simple test to detect antibodies in the
      blood which indicate an immunity to measles.  If the test shows a
      person lacking these antibodies, a vaccine can be administered to
      provide protection against the measles virus.  In order to determine
      the effectiveness of this new test it is administered to 500 people
      chosen at random.  An older more elaborate test reveals that 470 of
      the people have the measles antibodies.  The new test was positive
      when administered to 95% of those who have the antibodies and it
      also gave positive results in 6% of those who do not have them.
      Based on these results, what is the probability that a randomly
      chosen person has measles antibodies in his/her blood if the new
      test indicates their presence?

## Key Sheet - CHAPTER 8

[1]  $\frac{5}{8} = 0.63$

[2]  $\{7\}$

[3]  $\frac{9}{20} = 0.45$

[4]  0.79

[5]  P(at least one defective) = 0.78

[6]  $P(A \cup B) = 0.104$

[7]  4:3

[8]  $\frac{4}{9} \approx 0.44$

[9]  $\frac{130}{200} = 0.650$

[10] P(Tuesday and Thursday only) = 0.400

[11] $\frac{9}{37} \approx 0.243$

[12] No

[13] $\frac{36}{72} = 0.500$

[14] $P(A \cap B) = \frac{1}{4}$;  $P(A)P(B) = \left(\frac{1}{2}\right)\left(\frac{17}{32}\right) \neq \frac{1}{4}$
Events A and B are not independent.

[15] 0.12

[16] $\frac{15}{90} \approx 0.17$

[17] P(defective component) = 0.014

[18] $P(U_2 | R) = 0.17$

[19] $\frac{68}{83} \approx 0.82$

[20] 0.172

[21] P(measles antibodies | positive test) = 0.996

# DellenTest MAC 2.0
Copyright © 1995 by Prentice-Hall, Inc.

Essentials of College Mathematics, Third Edition
Raymond A. Barnett and Michael R. Ziegler

CHAPTER 8    Additional Topics in Probability

1.  A spinner is numbered from 1 through 10 with each number as likely to
    occur as any other.  Compute the probability that in a single spin the
    dial will stop at a number less than 5 or greater than 7.

2.  A box contains pieces of paper numbered 2 through 8.  An appropriate
    sample space is S = {2, 3, 4,..., 8}.  A single piece of paper is to
    be drawn.  Let event A = {2, 4, 6, 8} and let event B = {2, 3, 4, 5}.
    What is the event A' $\cup$ B?

3.  A survey of 100 students at a large university found that 85 students
    played tennis, 43 played basketball, and 35 played both tennis and
    basketball.  If a student is selected at random, what is the
    (empirical) probability that the student plays neither tennis nor
    basketball?

4.  A group of 10 people consists of 3 men and 7 women.  A committee of 4
    is chosen from this group.  What is the probability that one or more
    of the committee members is a man?

5.  A shipment of 28 compact disc players contains 3 that are
    defective.  If 7 players from this shipment are selected at
    random and tested, what is the probability that at least one
    defective player will be found?

6.  Two cards are randomly selected from a standard 52-card deck.  What
    is the probability of getting 2 hearts or 2 numbers less than 10
    (count aces as 1)?

7.  A spinner is numbered from 1 through 10 with each number as likely
    to occur as any other.  On a single spin what are the odds in favor of
    the pointer landing on an even number or a number divisible by 3?

8.  The odds in favor of event A are 2:4.  What is the probability of A'?

9.  Two groups of people were asked their preference in television
    programs from among three new programs.  The results are shown in the
    table below.  What is the probability that a person selected at random
    will be from group B or prefer program Y?

| Group of People | Television Program | | |
|---|---|---|---|
|  | X | Y | Z |
| A | 35 | 55 | 60 |
| B | 20 | 40 | 45 |

## CHAPTER 8   Additional Topics in Probability

10. From a survey involving 1,600 students at a large university, it was found that 1,300 students had classes on Monday, Wednesday, and Friday; 1,000 students had classes on Tuesday and Thursday; and 700 students had classes every day. If a student at this university is selected at random, what is the (empirical) probability that the student has classes only on Tuesday and Thursday?

11. A class of 50 students has 10 honor students and 13 athletes. Three of the honor students are also athletes. One student is chosen at random. Find the probability that this student is an athlete if it is known that the student is not an honor student.

12. A group of 25 people contains 10 brunettes, 8 blondes, and 7 redheads. Of the 15 girls in the group, 8 are brunettes, 6 are blondes, and 1 is a redhead. A person is selected at random. Are the events of being a girl and having brunette hair independent?

13. A box contains 4 red balls and 6 white balls. Two balls are to be drawn in succession without replacement. What is the probability that the sample will contain exactly one white ball and one red ball?

14. Suppose S is a sample space containing 140 equally likely simple events. Assume A and B are events in this sample space with the following properties: there are 20 simple events in A ∩ B; there are 20 simple events in A that are not in B; and there are 50 simple events in B that are not in A. Show why the events A and B are, or are not, independent.

15. Refer to the tree diagram below to find P(A and B').

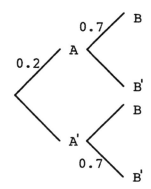

CHAPTER 8    Additional Topics in Probability

16. Each person in a group of students was identified by his or her hair color and then asked whether he or she preferred taking classes in the morning, afternoon, or evening. The results are shown in the table below. Find the probability that a student is a brunette given that he or she preferred afternoon classes.

| Class Time Preference | Hair Color | | |
| --- | --- | --- | --- |
| | Blonde | Brunette | Redhead |
| Morning | 20 | 5 | 15 |
| Afternoon | 45 | 35 | 40 |
| Evening | 10 | 25 | 50 |

17. In building the space shuttle, NASA contracts for certain guidance components to be supplied by three different companies: 41% by company A, 39% by company B, and 20% by company C. It has been found that 0.75%, 1.5%, and 1.75% of the components from companies A, B, and C, respectively, are defective. If one of these guidance components is selected at random, what is the probability that it is defective?

18. One urn has 4 red balls and 1 white balls; a second urn has 5 red balls and 3 white balls. A single card is randomly selected from a standard deck. If the card is less than 8 (aces count as 1), a ball is drawn out of the first urn; otherwise a ball is drawn out of the second urn. If the drawn ball is red, what is the probability that it came out of the first urn?

19. A small manufacturing company has rated 75% of its employees as satisfactory (S) and 25% as unsatisfactory (S'). Personnel records show that 80% of the satisfactory workers had previous work experience (E) in the job they are now doing, while 30% of the unsatisfactory workers had no work experience (E') in the job they are now doing. If a person who has had previous work experience is hired, what is the approximate empirical probability that this person will be an unsatisfactory employee?

20. A basketball team is to play two games in a tournament. The probability of winning the first game is 0.25. If the first game is won, the probability of winning the second game is 0.10. If the first game is lost, the probability of winning the second game is 0.15. What is the probability the first game was won if the second game is lost?

CHAPTER 8    Additional Topics in Probability

21. Due to the continuous growth in the number of cases of measles
    reported from several different locations around the country, a drug
    company has developed a new simple test to detect antibodies in the
    blood which indicate an immunity to measles.  If the test shows a
    person lacking these antibodies, a vaccine can be administered to
    provide protection against the measles virus.  In order to determine
    the effectiveness of this new test it is administered to 500 people
    chosen at random.  An older more elaborate test reveals that 445 of
    the people have the measles antibodies.  The new test was positive
    when administered to 97% of those who have the antibodies and it
    also gave positive results in 4% of those who do not have them.
    Based on these results, what is the probability that a randomly
    chosen person has measles antibodies in his/her blood if the new
    test indicates their presence?

## Key Sheet - CHAPTER 8

[1] $\frac{7}{10} = 0.70$

[2] {2, 3, 4, 5, 7}

[3] $\frac{7}{100} = 0.07$

[4] 0.83

[5] P(at least one defective) = 0.59

[6] P(A ∪ B) = 0.507

[7] 7:3

[8] $\frac{2}{3} \approx 0.67$

[9] $\frac{160}{255} \approx 0.627$

[10] P(Tuesday and Thursday only) = 0.188

[11] $\frac{1}{4} = 0.250$

[12] No

[13] $\frac{48}{90} \approx 0.533$

[14] $P(A \cap B) = \frac{1}{7}$; $P(A)P(B) = \left(\frac{2}{7}\right)\left(\frac{1}{2}\right) = \frac{1}{7}$
Events A and B are independent.

[15] 0.06

[16] $\frac{35}{120} \approx 0.29$

[17] P(defective component) = 0.012

[18] $P(U_1|R) = 0.60$

[19] $\frac{7}{31} \approx 0.23$

[20] 0.261

[21] P(measles antibodies|positive test) = 0.995

Essentials of College Mathematics, Third Edition
Raymond A. Barnett and Michael R. Ziegler

CHAPTER 8    Additional Topics in Probability

1.   A spinner is numbered from 1 through 9 with each number as likely to
     occur as any other.  Compute the probability that in a single spin the
     dial will stop at a number less than 3 or greater than 6.

2.   A box contains pieces of paper numbered 2 through 8.  An appropriate
     sample space is S = {2, 3, 4,..., 8}.  A single piece of paper is to
     be drawn.  Let event A = {2, 4, 6, 8} and let event B = {2, 3, 4, 5}.
     What is the event A' ∩ B' ?

3.   A survey of 100 students at a large university found that 85 students
     played tennis, 45 played basketball, and 40 played both tennis and
     basketball.  If a student is selected at random, what is the
     (empirical) probability that the student plays neither tennis nor
     basketball?

4.   A group of 11 people consists of 4 men and 7 women.  A committee of 4
     is chosen from this group.  What is the probability that one or more
     of the committee members is a man?

5.   A shipment of 35 compact disc players contains 9 that are
     defective.  If 7 players from this shipment are selected at
     random and tested, what is the probability that at least one
     defective player will be found?

6.   Two cards are randomly selected from a standard 52-card deck.  What
     is the probability of getting 2 hearts or 2 numbers less than 5
     (count aces as 1)?

7.   A spinner is numbered from 1 through 8 with each number as likely
     to occur as any other.  On a single spin what are the odds in favor of
     the pointer landing on an even number or a number divisible by 3?

8.   The odds in favor of event A are 4:5.  What is the probability of A'?

9.   Two groups of people were asked their preference in television
     programs from among three new programs.  The results are shown in the
     table below.  What is the probability that a person selected at random
     will be from group A or prefer program X?

| Group of People | Television Program | | |
|---|---|---|---|
| | X | Y | Z |
| A | 30 | 60 | 45 |
| B | 40 | 25 | 55 |

CHAPTER 8    Additional Topics in Probability

10.  From a survey involving 1,500 students at a large university, it
     was found that 500 students had classes on Monday, Wednesday, and
     Friday; 1,200 students had classes on Tuesday and Thursday; and 200
     students had classes every day.  If a student at this university
     is selected at random, what is the (empirical) probability that
     the student has classes only on Tuesday and Thursday?

11.  A class of 50 students has 12 honor students and 13 athletes.  Three
     of the honor students are also athletes.  One student is chosen at
     random.  Find the probability that this student is an athlete if it
     is known that the student is not an honor student.

12.  A group of 25 people contains 10 brunettes, 8 blondes, and 7 redheads.
     Of the 15 girls in the group, 6 are brunettes, 8 are blondes, and 1
     is a redhead.  A person is selected at random.  Are the events of
     being a girl and having brunette hair independent?

13.  A box contains 5 red balls and 3 white balls.  Two balls are to be
     drawn in succession without replacement.  What is the probability
     that the sample will contain exactly one white ball and one red ball?

14.  Suppose S is a sample space containing 80 equally likely simple
     events.  Assume A and B are events in this sample space with the
     following properties: there are 10 simple events in A ∩ B; there
     are 10 simple events in A that are not in B; and there are 35
     simple events in B that are not in A.  Show why the events A and B
     are, or are not, independent.

15.  Refer to the tree diagram below to find P(A and B').

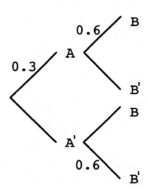

CHAPTER 8    Additional Topics in Probability

16. Each person in a group of students was identified by his or her hair color and then asked whether he or she preferred taking classes in the morning, afternoon, or evening. The results are shown in the table below. Find the probability that a student preferred morning classes given he or she has blonde hair.

| Class Time Preference | Hair Color | | |
|---|---|---|---|
| | Blonde | Brunette | Redhead |
| Morning | 35 | 40 | 45 |
| Afternoon | 25 | 10 | 50 |
| Evening | 30 | 5 | 15 |

17. In building the space shuttle, NASA contracts for certain guidance components to be supplied by three different companies: 43% by company A, 38% by company B, and 19% by company C. It has been found that 1%, 0.75%, and 1.25% of the components from companies A, B, and C, respectively, are defective. If one of these guidance components is selected at random, what is the probability that it is defective?

18. One urn has 4 red balls and 2 white balls; a second urn has 2 red balls and 6 white balls. A single card is randomly selected from a standard deck. If the card is less than 6 (aces count as 1), a ball is drawn out of the first urn; otherwise a ball is drawn out of the second urn. If the drawn ball is red, what is the probability that it came out of the first urn?

19. A small manufacturing company has rated 80% of its employees as satisfactory (S) and 20% as unsatisfactory (S'). Personnel records show that 70% of the satisfactory workers had previous work experience (E) in the job they are now doing, while 25% of the unsatisfactory workers had no work experience (E') in the job they are now doing. If a person who has had no previous work experience is hired, what is the approximate empirical probability that this person will be a satisfactory employee?

20. A basketball team is to play two games in a tournament. The probability of winning the first game is 0.15. If the first game is won, the probability of winning the second game is 0.20. If the first game is lost, the probability of winning the second game is 0.30. What is the probability the first game was won if the second game is lost?

CHAPTER 8    Additional Topics in Probability

21.  Due to the continuous growth in the number of cases of measles
     reported from several different locations around the country, a drug
     company has developed a new simple test to detect antibodies in the
     blood which indicate an immunity to measles.  If the test shows a
     person lacking these antibodies, a vaccine can be administered to
     provide protection against the measles virus.  In order to determine
     the effectiveness of this new test it is administered to 500 people
     chosen at random.  An older more elaborate test reveals that 465 of
     the people have the measles antibodies.  The new test was positive
     when administered to 96% of those who have the antibodies and it
     also gave positive results in 3% of those who do not have them.
     Based on these results, what is the probability that a randomly
     chosen person has measles antibodies in his/her blood if the new
     test indicates their presence?

## Key Sheet - CHAPTER 8

[1]  $\frac{5}{9} = 0.56$

[2]  {7}

[3]  $\frac{1}{10} = 0.10$

[4]  0.89

[5]  P(at least one defective) = 0.90

[6]  P(A ∪ B) = 0.145

[7]  5:3

[8]  $\frac{5}{9} \approx 0.56$

[9]  $\frac{175}{255} \approx 0.686$

[10]  P(Tuesday and Thursday only) = 0.667

[11]  $\frac{5}{19} \approx 0.263$

[12]  Yes

[13]  $\frac{30}{56} \approx 0.536$

[14]  $P(A \cap B) = \frac{1}{8}$;  $P(A)P(B) = \left(\frac{1}{4}\right)\left(\frac{9}{16}\right) \neq \frac{1}{8}$
Events A and B are not independent.

[15]  0.12

[16]  $\frac{35}{90} \approx 0.39$

[17]  P(defective component) = 0.010

[18]  $P(U_1 | R) = 0.63$

[19]  $\frac{24}{29} \approx 0.83$

[20]  0.168

[21]  P(measles antibodies | positive test) = 0.998

# DellenTest MAC 2.0

Copyright © 1995 by Prentice-Hall, Inc.

Essentials of College Mathematics, Third Edition
Raymond A. Barnett and Michael R. Ziegler

Form A-A                                                         Page 1

---

CHAPTER 9    The Derivative

---

1.    Use the graph to estimate $\lim\limits_{x \to -1} g(x)$.

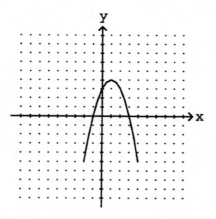

2.    Determine where $f(x) = \dfrac{x + 2}{(x - 5)(x - 3)}$ is continuous.

3.    Use the graph to estimate $\lim\limits_{x \to -1^+} f(x)$.

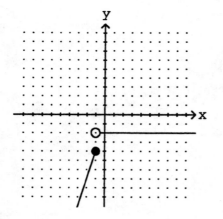

---

CHAPTER 9    The Derivative

---

4.  Refer to the graph of f(x) below:
    (a) Find: f(1)
    (b) Find:  lim  f(x)
              x → 1
    (c) Is f(x) continuous at x = 1?

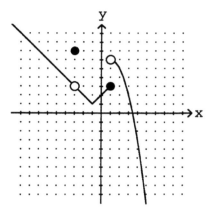

5.  Where is $f(x) = \sqrt{6 - x}$ continuous?  Express answer in interval notation.

6.  Express Package Delivery Service uses the weight of a package to determine the charge for delivery.  The charge is $9 for the first pound (or any fraction thereof) and $3 for each additional pound (or fraction thereof) up to 9 pounds.  If C(x) is the charge for delivering a package weighing x pounds, then

$$C(x) = \begin{cases} 9 & \text{for } 0 < x \le 1 \\ 12 & \text{for } 1 < x \le 2 \\ 15 & \text{for } 2 < x \le 3 \\ \text{and so on.} \end{cases}$$

    Graph C for $0 < x \le 4$.

7.  Given $\lim_{x \to 5} f(x) = 2$ and $\lim_{x \to 5} g(x) = 7$, find $\lim_{x \to 5} \dfrac{2f(x) + 5g(x)}{4f(x)}$.

8.  Find: $\lim_{x \to 2} \dfrac{x - 2}{x^2 - 5x + 6}$

9.  Find: $\lim_{x \to -\infty} \dfrac{3x^2 + 4}{2x^3}$

10. Find: $\lim_{x \to 6} \dfrac{3x - 1}{7x + 9}$

## CHAPTER 9    The Derivative

11.  Find:  $\lim\limits_{x \to 5^+} \dfrac{5x}{x - 5}$.  Use $-\infty$ or $\infty$ where appropriate.

12.  Use the graph to find $\lim\limits_{x \to -3^+} f(x)$.  Use $-\infty$ or $\infty$ where appropriate.

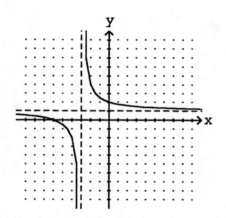

13.  Use the graph to find $\lim\limits_{x \to \infty} f(x)$:

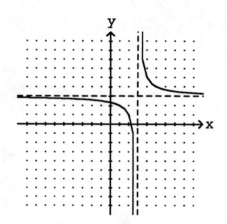

14.  The concentration of caffeine found in Mr. Cole's bloodstream
     t minutes after finishing his morning cup of coffee is given by:

$$C(t) = \frac{2t}{9 + t}$$

Find $\lim\limits_{t \to \infty} C(t)$.

## CHAPTER 9    The Derivative

15. Find the slope of the secant line joining $(-2, f(-2))$ and $(0, f(0))$ for $f(x) = 3x^2 - 3$.

16. Find $\lim\limits_{h \to 0} \dfrac{f(8 + h) - f(8)}{h}$ for $f(x) = -4x + 7$.

17. Given $f(x + h) - f(x) = 10xh + 3h + 5h^2$, find the slope of the tangent line at $x = 1$.

18. Use the two-step method to find $f'(x)$ for $f(x) = 2x^2 + 7x$. Show your work.

19. Find $f'(x)$ for $f(x) = -3x^5 + 8x^8$.

20. Find: $D_x \left[ \dfrac{3}{x^4} + 5 \sqrt[4]{x} \right]$

21. Find the equation of the tangent line at $x = -1$ for: $f(x) = -3 - x + 4x^2 - 4x^3$. Write the answer in the form $y = mx + b$.

22. Find the values of $x$ where the tangent line is horizontal for $f(x) = 8x^3 - x^2 + 9$.

23. An object moves along the y-axis (marked in feet) so that its position at time t in seconds is:

    $f(t) = 5t^3 - 2t^2 - 6t + 16$

    Find the velocity at 2 seconds.

24. A sponge manufacturer determined that the total cost in dollars of producing x dozen sponges in one day is:

    $C(x) = 100 + 2x - 0.02x^2$

    Find the marginal cost at a production level of 40 dozen sponges and interpret.

25. According to one theory of learning, the number of items $w(t)$ that a person can learn after t hours of instruction is given by:

    $w(t) = 15 \sqrt[3]{t^2}, \quad 0 \le t \le 125$

    Find the rate of learning at the end of 8 hours of instruction.

26. Find $f'(x)$ for $f(x) = \dfrac{9x + 7}{5x + 8}$.

27. Find $f'(x)$ for $f(x) = (-5x^7 + x^3)(4x^2 - 2x - 3)$. Do not simplify.

CHAPTER 9    The Derivative

28. Find $\frac{dy}{dx}$ for $y = \frac{-4x^4 - 5x^2 + 2}{x^3 - 4}$. Do not simplify.

29. Find the values of x where the tangent line is horizontal for the graph of $f(x) = \frac{2x^2}{4x + 1}$.

30. One hour after x milligrams of a particular drug are given to a person, the change in body temperature T(x) in degrees Celsius is given approximately by:

$$T(x) = \frac{5x^2}{9}\left(1 - \frac{x}{9}\right) - \frac{160}{9} \qquad 0 \le x \le 6$$

Find the sensitivity, T'(x), of the body to a dosage of 2 milligrams.

31. A publishing company has published a new magazine for young adults. The monthly sales S (in thousands) is given by

$$S(t) = \frac{700t}{t + 1}$$

where t is the number of months since the first issue was published. Find S(4) and S'(4) and interpret.

32. Find $f'(x)$ for $f(x) = (4x + 9)^{-6}$.

33. Find $D_x y$ for $y = (x^2 + 4x)^5$.

34. Find: $D_x \sqrt[6]{6x^5 - 16}$

35. Find $D_x y$ for $y = \frac{(2x + 1)^2}{x^5 + 4x^3 - 2x}$. Do not simplify.

36. The total cost in hundreds of dollars of producing x radios per day is given by:

$$C(x) = 13 + \sqrt{3x + 25}, \quad 0 \le x \le 50$$

Find the marginal cost at x = 13 and interpret.

37. The total cost in dollars of producing x lawn mowers is:

$$C(x) = 3,500 + 90x - \frac{x^2}{3}$$

Find the marginal average cost at x = 20, $\overline{C}'(20)$, and interpret.

38. The demand equation for a certain item is $p = 14 - \frac{x}{1,000}$ and the cost equation is $C(x) = 5,000 + 7x$. Find the marginal profit at a production level of 5,000 and interpret.

CHAPTER 9    The Derivative

39. The total cost in dollars of producing x coffee makers is:

$$C(x) = 5,000 + 40x - \frac{x^2}{2}$$

Find the exact cost of producing the 21st coffee maker.

40. A company is planning to manufacture a new blender. After conducting
extensive market surveys, the research department estimates a weekly
demand of 500 blenders at a price of $50 per blender and a weekly
demand of 600 blenders at a price of $30 per blender. Assuming the
demand equation is linear, use the research department's estimates
to find the revenue equation in terms of the demand x.

41. The market research department of a company recommends that the
company manufacture steam irons. After suitable test marketing, the
research department presents the following demand equation

$$p = 18 - \frac{x}{50}$$

where x is the number of irons retailers are likely to buy per week
at $p. The financial department provides the following cost equation

$$C(x) = 1,200 + 4x$$

where $1,200 is the estimated fixed costs and $4 is the
estimated variable costs. Graph the revenue and cost equations, and
find the break-even points.

## Key Sheet - CHAPTER 9

[1]   0

[2]   all x, except x = 5 and x = 3

[3]   -2

      (a) 3
      (b) Does not exist
[4]   (c) No

[5]   (−∞, 6]

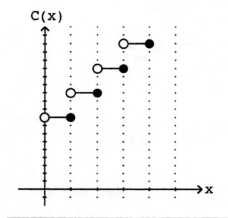

[6]

[7]   $\frac{39}{8}$

[8]   -1

[9]   0

[10]  $\frac{1}{3}$

[11]  ∞

[12]  ∞

[13]  3

[14]  2

[15]  -6

[16]  -4

Key Sheet - CHAPTER 9

[17]  13

Step 1:
$$\frac{f(x + h) - f(x)}{h} = \frac{[2(x + h)^2 + 7(x + h)] - [2x^2 + 7x]}{h}$$

$$= \frac{2x^2 + 4hx + 2h^2 + 7x + 7h - 2x^2 - 7x}{h}$$

$$= \frac{4hx + 2h^2 + 7h}{h} = 4x + 2h + 7, \; h \neq 0$$

Step 2:
$$f'(x) = \lim_{h \to 0} \frac{f(x + h) - f(x)}{h}$$

$$= \lim_{h \to 0} 4x + 2h + 7 = 4x + 7$$

[18]

[19]  $-15x^4 + 64x^7$

[20]  $-12x^{-5} + \frac{5}{4}(x)^{-3/4}$ or $-\frac{12}{x^5} + \frac{5}{4\sqrt[4]{x^3}}$

[21]  $y = -21x - 15$

[22]  $x = 0, \; x = \frac{1}{12}$

[23]  46 ft/sec

[24]  The marginal cost is $0.40/doz.
The cost of producing one dozen more sponges at a production level of 40 dozen sponges is approximately $0.40.

[25]  5 items per hour

[26]  $\dfrac{37}{(5x + 8)^2}$

[27]  $(-5x^7 + x^3)(8x - 2) + (-35x^6 + 3x^2)(4x^2 - 2x - 3)$

[28]  $\dfrac{(x^3 - 4)(-16x^3 - 10x) - (-4x^4 - 5x^2 + 2)(3x^2)}{(x^3 - 4)^2}$

[29]  $x = 0, \; x = -\frac{1}{2}$

## Key Sheet - CHAPTER 9

[30] $\frac{40}{27}$ degrees per milligrams

[31] At 4 months, the monthly sales are 560,000 and increasing at 28,000 magazines per month.

[32] $\frac{-24}{(4x + 9)^7}$

[33] $5(x^2 + 4x)^4(2x + 4)$

[34] $\frac{5x^4}{(6x^5 - 16)^{5/6}}$ or $\frac{5x^4}{6\sqrt{(6x^5 - 16)^5}}$

[35] $\frac{4(x^5 + 4x^3 - 2x)(2x + 1) - (2x + 1)^2(5x^4 + 12x^2 - 2)}{(x^5 + 4x^3 - 2x)^2}$

[36] The marginal cost is $18.75. The cost of producing one more radio at this level of production is approximately $18.75.

[37] -$9.08; A unit increase in production will decrease the average cost per unit by approximately $9.08 at a production level of 20 units.

[38] -$3; At the 5,000 level of production, profit will decrease by approximately -$3 for each unit increase in production.

[39] $19.50

[40] $R(x) = 150x - \frac{x^2}{5}$

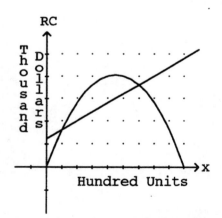

[41] Break-even points: (100, 1,600) and (600, 3,600)

## CHAPTER 9    The Derivative

1.    Use the graph to estimate $\lim\limits_{x \to -1} g(x)$.

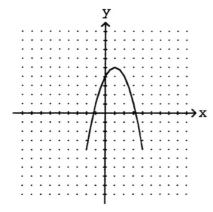

2.    Determine where $f(x) = \dfrac{x + 5}{(x - 1)(x + 1)}$ is continuous.

3.    Use the graph to estimate $\lim\limits_{x \to 4^-} f(x)$.

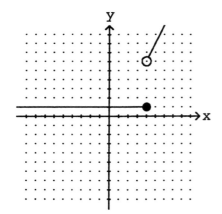

## CHAPTER 9    The Derivative

4.    Refer to the graph of f(x) below:
      (a) Find: f(3)
      (b) Find:  lim  f(x)
                x → 3
      (c) Is f(x) continuous at x = 3?

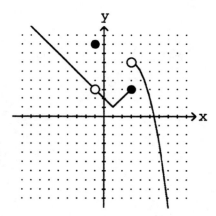

5.    Where is $f(x) = \sqrt{13 - x}$ continuous?  Express answer in interval notation.

6.    Express Package Delivery Service uses the weight of a package to determine the charge for delivery.  The charge is $5 for the first pound (or any fraction thereof) and $3 for each additional pound (or fraction thereof) up to 8 pounds.  If C(x) is the charge for delivering a package weighing x pounds, then

$$C(x) = \begin{cases} 5 & \text{for } 0 < x \le 1 \\ 8 & \text{for } 1 < x \le 2 \\ 11 & \text{for } 2 < x \le 3 \\ \text{and so on.} \end{cases}$$

Graph C for $0 < x \le 5$.

7.    Given $\lim\limits_{x \to 2} f(x) = 1$ and $\lim\limits_{x \to 2} g(x) = 8$, find $\lim\limits_{x \to 2} \dfrac{2f(x) + 3g(x)}{3f(x)}$.

8.    Find: $\lim\limits_{x \to 3} \dfrac{x - 3}{x^2 - 6x + 9}$

9.    Find: $\lim\limits_{x \to -\infty} \dfrac{5x^4 + 5}{x^4}$

10.   Find: $\lim\limits_{x \to -4} \dfrac{9x + 4}{5x - 9}$

CHAPTER 9    The Derivative

11.  Find: $\lim\limits_{x \to -2^{+}} \dfrac{8x}{x + 2}$.  Use $-\infty$ or $\infty$ where appropriate.

12.  Use the graph to find $\lim\limits_{x \to 1^{-}} f(x)$.  Use $-\infty$ or $\infty$ where appropriate.

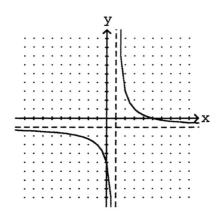

13.  Use the graph to find $\lim\limits_{x \to \infty} f(x)$:

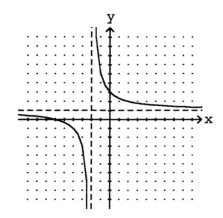

14.  The concentration of caffeine found in Mr. Brown's bloodstream
     t minutes after finishing his morning cup of coffee is given by:

$$C(t) = \frac{4t}{t^2 + 9}$$

Find $\lim\limits_{t \to \infty} C(t)$.

## CHAPTER 9    The Derivative

15. Find the slope of the secant line joining $(2, f(2))$ and $(3, f(3))$ for $f(x) = 3x^2 - 2$.

16. Find $\lim\limits_{h \to 0} \dfrac{f(7 + h) - f(7)}{h}$ for $f(x) = -6x + 3$.

17. Given $f(x + h) - f(x) = 2xh + 5h + h^2$, find the slope of the tangent line at $x = 5$.

18. Use the two-step method to find $f'(x)$ for $f(x) = 3x^2 - 4x$. Show your work.

19. Find $f'(x)$ for $f(x) = 8x^5 + 3x^8$.

20. Find: $D_x \left[ \dfrac{5}{x^5} + 3 \sqrt[4]{x} \right]$

21. Find the equation of the tangent line at $x = -2$ for:
    $f(x) = -1 + 4x + 2x^2 + 3x^3$.  Write the answer in the form $y = mx + b$.

22. Find the values of $x$ where the tangent line is horizontal for
    $f(x) = 7x^3 + x^2 - 5$.

23. An object moves along the y-axis (marked in feet) so that its position at time t in seconds is:

    $f(t) = t^3 - 7t^2 - 3t + 17$

    Find the velocity at 7 seconds.

24. A ball manufacturer determined that the total cost in dollars of producing x dozen balls in one day is:

    $C(x) = 100 + 4x - 0.02x^2$

    Find the marginal cost at a production level of 60 dozen balls and interpret.

25. According to one theory of learning, the number of items w(t) that a person can learn after t hours of instruction is given by:

    $w(t) = 39 \sqrt[3]{t^2}, \quad 0 \le t \le 64$

    Find the rate of learning at the end of 27 hours of instruction.

26. Find $f'(x)$ for $f(x) = \dfrac{6x - 5}{7x - 8}$.

27. Find $f'(x)$ for $f(x) = (-4x^5 + 2x^4)(6x^2 - 6x + 4)$.  Do not simplify.

## CHAPTER 9    The Derivative

28.  Find $\frac{dy}{dx}$ for $y = \frac{-5x^4 + 5x^3 - 3}{x + 1}$.  Do not simplify.

29.  Find the values of x where the tangent line is horizontal for the
     graph of $f(x) = \frac{3x^2}{x + 2}$.

30.  One hour after x milligrams of a particular drug are given to a
     person, the change in body temperature T(x) in degrees Celsius is
     given approximately by:
     $$T(x) = \frac{5x^2}{9}\left(1 - \frac{x}{9}\right) - \frac{160}{9} \quad 0 \le x \le 6$$
     Find the sensitivity, T'(x), of the body to a dosage of 3 milligrams.

31.  A publishing company has published a new magazine for young adults.
     The monthly sales S (in thousands) is given by
     $$S(t) = \frac{900t}{t + 8}$$
     where t is the number of months since the first issue was published.
     Find S(2) and S'(2) and interpret.

32.  Find f'(x) for $f(x) = (2x - 3)^{-6}$.

33.  Find $D_x y$ for $y = (3x^4 + x^2)^2$.

34.  Find: $D_x \sqrt[5]{5x^5 - 10}$

35.  Find $D_x y$ for $y = \frac{(3x - 1)^5}{x^3 - x^2 - 4x}$.  Do not simplify.

36.  The total cost in hundreds of dollars of producing x cameras per
     day is given by:
     $$C(x) = 32 + \sqrt{3x + 4}, \quad 0 \le x \le 50$$
     Find the marginal cost at x = 32 and interpret.

37.  The total cost in dollars of producing x lawn mowers is:
     $$C(x) = 4,000 + 110x - \frac{x^2}{2}$$
     Find the marginal average cost at x = 10, $\overline{C}'(10)$, and interpret.

38.  The demand equation for a certain item is $p = 12 - \frac{x}{1,000}$ and the cost
     equation is C(x) = 4,000 + 3x.  Find the marginal profit at a
     production level of 1,000 and interpret.

## CHAPTER 9    The Derivative

39. The total cost in dollars of producing x coffee makers is:

$$C(x) = 3,000 + 60x - \frac{x^2}{5}$$

Find the exact cost of producing the 91st coffee maker.

40. A company is planning to manufacture a new blender. After conducting extensive market surveys, the research department estimates a weekly demand of 600 blenders at a price of $40 per blender and a weekly demand of 800 blenders at a price of $20 per blender. Assuming the demand equation is linear, use the research department's estimates to find the revenue equation in terms of the demand x.

41. The market research department of a company recommends that the company manufacture steam irons. After suitable test marketing, the research department presents the following demand equation

$$p = 17 - \frac{x}{50}$$

where x is the number of irons retailers are likely to buy per week at $p. The financial department provides the following cost equation

$$C(x) = 2,000 + 3x$$

where $2,000 is the estimated fixed costs and $3 is the estimated variable costs. Graph the revenue and cost equations, and find the break-even points.

Key Sheet - CHAPTER 9

[1]  1

[2]  all x, except x = 1 and x = -1

[3]  1

[4]  (a) 3
     (b) Does not exist
     (c) No

[5]  (-∞, 13]

[6]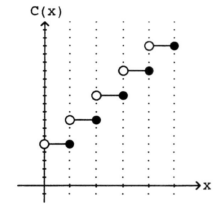

[7]  $\dfrac{26}{3}$

[8]  Limit does not exist

[9]  5

[10] $\dfrac{32}{29}$

[11] -∞

[12] -∞

[13] 1

[14] 0

[15] 15

[16] -6

## Key Sheet - CHAPTER 9

[17] 15

Step 1:
$$\frac{f(x + h) - f(x)}{h} = \frac{[3(x + h)^2 - 4(x + h)] - [3x^2 - 4x]}{h}$$

$$= \frac{3x^2 + 6hx + 3h^2 - 4x - 4h - 3x^2 + 4x}{h}$$

$$= \frac{6hx + 3h^2 - 4h}{h} = 6x + 3h - 4, \ h \neq 0$$

Step 2:
$$f'(x) = \lim_{h \to 0} \frac{f(x + h) - f(x)}{h}$$

$$= \lim_{h \to 0} 6x + 3h - 4 = 6x - 4$$

[18]

[19] $40x^4 + 24x^7$

[20] $-25x^{-6} + \frac{3}{4}(x)^{-3/4}$ or $-\frac{25}{x^6} + \frac{3}{4\sqrt[4]{x^3}}$

[21] $y = 32x + 39$

[22] $x = 0, \ x = -\frac{2}{21}$

[23] 46 ft/sec

[24] The marginal cost is \$1.60/doz.
The cost of producing one dozen more balls at a production level of 60 dozen balls is approximately \$1.60.

[25] $8\frac{2}{3}$ items per hour

[26] $\frac{-13}{(7x - 8)^2}$

[27] $(-4x^5 + 2x^4)(12x - 6) + (-20x^4 + 8x^3)(6x^2 - 6x + 4)$

[28] $\frac{(x + 1)(-20x^3 + 15x^2) - (-5x^4 + 5x^3 - 3)(1)}{(x + 1)^2}$

[29] $x = 0, \ x = -4$

Key Sheet - CHAPTER 9

[30] $\frac{5}{3}$ degrees per milligrams

[31] At 2 months, the monthly sales are 180,000 and increasing at 72,000 magazines per month.

[32] $\dfrac{-12}{(2x - 3)^7}$

[33] $2(3x^4 + x^2)(12x^3 + 2x)$

[34] $\dfrac{5x^4}{(5x^5 - 10)^{4/5}}$ or $\dfrac{5x^4}{5\sqrt{(5x^5 - 10)^4}}$

[35] $\dfrac{15(x^3 - x^2 - 4x)(3x - 1)^4 - (3x - 1)^5(3x^2 - 2x - 4)}{(x^3 - x^2 - 4x)^2}$

[36] The marginal cost is $15.00. The cost of producing one more camera at this level of production is approximately $15.00.

[37] -$40.50; A unit increase in production will decrease the average cost per unit by approximately $40.50 at a production level of 10 units.

[38] $7; At the 1,000 level of production, profit will increase by approximately $7 for each unit increase in production.

[39] $23.80

[40] $R(x) = 100x - \dfrac{x^2}{10}$

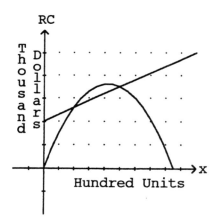

[41] Break-even points: (200, 2,600) and (500, 3,500)

CHAPTER 9    The Derivative

1.    Use the graph to estimate $\lim\limits_{x \to 6}$ g(x).

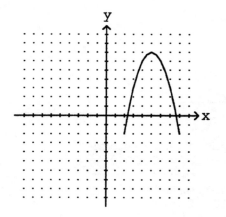

2.    Determine where $f(x) = \dfrac{x - 4}{(x - 1)(x + 3)}$ is continuous.

3.    Use the graph to estimate $\lim\limits_{x \to 1^-}$ f(x).

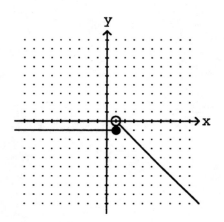

CHAPTER 9    The Derivative

4.    Refer to the graph of f(x) below:
      (a) Find: f(4)
      (b) Find:  lim  f(x)
                 x → 4
      (c) Is f(x) continuous at x = 4?

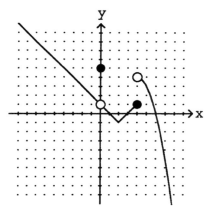

5.    Where is $f(x) = \sqrt{4 - x}$ continuous?  Express answer in interval notation.

6.    Express Package Delivery Service uses the weight of a package to determine the charge for delivery.  The charge is $6 for the first pound (or any fraction thereof) and $3 for each additional pound (or fraction thereof) up to 10 pounds.  If C(x) is the charge for delivering a package weighing x pounds, then

$$C(x) = \begin{cases} 6 & \text{for } 0 < x \le 1 \\ 9 & \text{for } 1 < x \le 2 \\ 12 & \text{for } 2 < x \le 3 \\ \text{and so on.} \end{cases}$$

      Graph C for $0 < x \le 4$.

7.    Given $\lim_{x \to 6} f(x) = -5$ and $\lim_{x \to 6} g(x) = -4$, find $\lim_{x \to 6} \dfrac{5f(x) + 2g(x)}{3f(x)}$.

8.    Find: $\lim_{x \to 4} \dfrac{x - 4}{x^2 - 8x + 16}$

9.    Find: $\lim_{x \to \infty} \dfrac{x^2 + 1}{3x^4}$

10.   Find: $\lim_{x \to -5} \dfrac{7x - 6}{6x + 5}$

---

## CHAPTER 9    The Derivative

---

11.  Find: $\lim\limits_{x \to 5^+} \dfrac{3x}{x - 5}$.  Use $-\infty$ or $\infty$ where appropriate.

12.  Use the graph to find $\lim\limits_{x \to 2^+} f(x)$.  Use $-\infty$ or $\infty$ where appropriate.

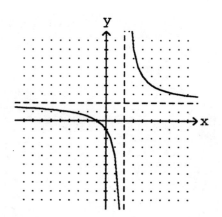

13.  Use the graph to find $\lim\limits_{x \to \infty} f(x)$:

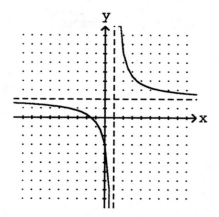

14.  The concentration of caffeine found in Mr. Brown's bloodstream
     t minutes after finishing his morning cup of coffee is given by:

$$C(t) = \frac{3t}{9 + t}$$

     Find $\lim\limits_{t \to \infty} C(t)$.

---

CHAPTER 9     The Derivative

---

15.  Find the slope of the secant line joining $(-1, f(-1))$ and $(0, f(0))$
     for $f(x) = 5x^2 + 1$.

16.  Find $\lim\limits_{h \to 0} \dfrac{f(3 + h) - f(3)}{h}$ for $f(x) = 7x + 2$.

17.  Given $f(x + h) - f(x) = 8xh + 3h + 4h^2$, find the slope of the
     tangent line at $x = 5$.

18.  Use the two-step method to find $f'(x)$ for $f(x) = 7x^2 + 3x$.
     Show your work.

19.  Find $f'(x)$ for $f(x) = -2x^3 - 6x^8$.

20.  Find: $D_x \left[ \dfrac{-3}{x^3} + 4 \sqrt[4]{x} \right]$

21.  Find the equation of the tangent line at $x = 0$ for:
     $f(x) = -4 + 3x - x^2 + 2x^3$.  Write the answer in the form $y = mx + b$.

22.  Find the values of $x$ where the tangent line is horizontal for
     $f(x) = 6x^3 - 5x^2 + 2$.

23.  An object moves along the y-axis (marked in feet) so that its
     position at time t in seconds is:

     $f(t) = 3t^3 + t^2 + 3t + 13$

     Find the velocity at 9 seconds.

24.  A pen manufacturer determined that the total cost in dollars of
     producing x dozen pens in one day is:

     $C(x) = 500 + 3x - 0.01x^2$

     Find the marginal cost at a production level of 60 dozen pens
     and interpret.

25.  According to one theory of learning, the number of items w(t) that
     a person can learn after t hours of instruction is given by:

     $w(t) = 21 \sqrt[3]{t^2}, \quad 0 \le t \le 125$

     Find the rate of learning at the end of 64 hours of instruction.

26.  Find $f'(x)$ for $f(x) = \dfrac{4x - 9}{8x - 7}$.

27.  Find $f'(x)$ for $f(x) = (5x^7 + x^5)(3x^2 + 4x - 5)$.  Do not simplify.

## CHAPTER 9    The Derivative

28. Find $\frac{dy}{dx}$ for $y = \frac{5x^5 - 5x + 5}{4x^3 + 3}$. Do not simplify.

29. Find the values of $x$ where the tangent line is horizontal for the graph of $f(x) = \frac{x^2}{4x + 3}$.

30. One hour after $x$ milligrams of a particular drug are given to a person, the change in body temperature $T(x)$ in degrees Celsius is given approximately by:

    $$T(x) = \frac{5x^2}{9}\left(1 - \frac{x}{9}\right) - \frac{160}{9} \quad 0 \leq x \leq 6$$

    Find the sensitivity, $T'(x)$, of the body to a dosage of 1 milligram.

31. A publishing company has published a new magazine for young adults. The monthly sales $S$ (in thousands) is given by

    $$S(t) = \frac{800t}{3t + 1}$$

    where $t$ is the number of months since the first issue was published. Find $S(3)$ and $S'(3)$ and interpret.

32. Find $f'(x)$ for $f(x) = (7x - 5)^{-3}$.

33. Find $D_x y$ for $y = (4x^4 - x^2)^4$.

34. Find: $D_x \sqrt[6]{6x^5 - 16}$

35. Find $D_x y$ for $y = \frac{(5x + 2)^5}{x^5 + 2x^4 + x^2}$. Do not simplify.

36. The total cost in hundreds of dollars of producing $x$ dolls per day is given by:

    $$C(x) = 14 + \sqrt{3x + 22}, \quad 0 \leq x \leq 50$$

    Find the marginal cost at $x = 14$ and interpret.

37. The total cost in dollars of producing $x$ lawn mowers is:

    $$C(x) = 3,000 + 90x - \frac{x^2}{3}$$

    Find the marginal average cost at $x = 40$, $\overline{C}'(40)$, and interpret.

38. The demand equation for a certain item is $p = 13 - \frac{x}{1,000}$ and the cost equation is $C(x) = 4,000 + 4x$. Find the marginal profit at a production level of 2,000 and interpret.

## CHAPTER 9   The Derivative

39. The total cost in dollars of producing x coffee makers is:

$$C(x) = 1,000 + 60x - \frac{x^2}{4}$$

Find the exact cost of producing the 31st coffee maker.

40. A company is planning to manufacture a new blender. After conducting extensive market surveys, the research department estimates a weekly demand of 300 blenders at a price of $50 per blender and a weekly demand of 400 blenders at a price of $30 per blender. Assuming the demand equation is linear, use the research department's estimates to find the revenue equation in terms of the demand x.

41. The market research department of a company recommends that the company manufacture steam irons. After suitable test marketing, the research department presents the following demand equation

$$p = 20 - \frac{x}{50}$$

where x is the number of irons retailers are likely to buy per week at $p. The financial department provides the following cost equation

$$C(x) = 3,600 + 2x$$

where $3,600 is the estimated fixed costs and $2 is the estimated variable costs. Graph the revenue and cost equations, and find the break-even points.

## Key Sheet – CHAPTER 9

[1]  6

[2]  all x, except x = 1 and x = -3

[3]  -1

(a) 1
(b) Does not exist
[4]  (c) No

[5]  (−∞, 4]

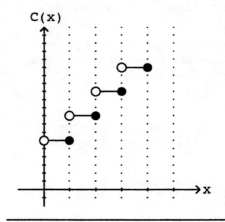

[6]

[7]  $\dfrac{11}{5}$

[8]  Limit does not exist

[9]  0

[10]  $\dfrac{41}{25}$

[11]  ∞

[12]  ∞

[13]  2

[14]  3

[15]  -5

[16]  7

Key Sheet - CHAPTER 9

[17] 43

Step 1:
$$\frac{f(x + h) - f(x)}{h} = \frac{[7(x + h)^2 + 3(x + h)] - [7x^2 + 3x]}{h}$$

$$= \frac{7x^2 + 14hx + 7h^2 + 3x + 3h - 7x^2 - 3x}{h}$$

$$= \frac{14hx + 7h^2 + 3h}{h} = 14x + 7h + 3, \ h \neq 0$$

Step 2:
$$f'(x) = \lim_{h \to 0} \frac{f(x + h) - f(x)}{h}$$

$$= \lim_{h \to 0} 14x + 7h + 3 = 14x + 3$$
[18]

[19] $-6x^2 - 48x^7$

[20] $9x^{-4} + (x)^{-3/4}$ or $\dfrac{9}{x^4} + \dfrac{1}{4\sqrt{x^3}}$

[21] $y = 3x - 4$

[22] $x = 0, \ x = \dfrac{5}{9}$

[23] 750 ft/sec

[24] The marginal cost is \$1.80/doz.
The cost of producing one dozen more pens at a production level of 60 dozen pens is approximately \$1.80.

[25] $3\frac{1}{2}$ items per hour

[26] $\dfrac{44}{(8x - 7)^2}$

[27] $(5x^7 + x^5)(6x + 4) + (35x^6 + 5x^4)(3x^2 + 4x - 5)$

[28] $\dfrac{(4x^3 + 3)(25x^4 - 5) - (5x^5 - 5x + 5)(12x^2)}{(4x^3 + 3)^2}$

[29] $x = 0, \ x = -\dfrac{3}{2}$

[30] $\dfrac{25}{27}$ degrees per milligrams

[31] At 3 months, the monthly sales are 240,000 and increasing at 8,000 magazines per month.

[32] $\dfrac{-21}{(7x - 5)^4}$

[33] $4(4x^4 - x^2)^3(16x^3 - 2x)$

[34] $\dfrac{5x^4}{(6x^5 - 16)^{5/6}}$ or $\dfrac{5x^4}{\sqrt[6]{(6x^5 - 16)^5}}$

[35] $\dfrac{25(x^5 + 2x^4 + x^2)(5x + 2)^4 - (5x + 2)^5(5x^4 + 8x^3 + 2x)}{(x^5 + 2x^4 + x^2)^2}$

[36] The marginal cost is $18.75. The cost of producing one more doll at this level of production is approximately $18.75.

[37] -$2.21; A unit increase in production will decrease the average cost per unit by approximately $2.21 at a production level of 40 units.

[38] $5; At the 2,000 level of production, profit will increase by approximately $5 for each unit increase in production.

[39] $44.75

[40] $R(x) = 110x - \dfrac{x^2}{5}$

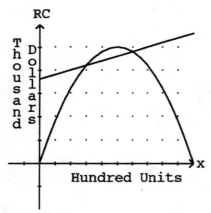

[41] Break-even points: (300, 4,200) and (600, 4,800)

CHAPTER 10    Additional Derivative Topics

1.  Solve the inequality: $x^2 + x - 6 \leq 0$

2.  Given $f(x) = 2x^3 - 9x^2 + 5$, for which values of x is $f(x)$ decreasing?

3.  The critical values of $f(x) = 4x^3 - 48x + 24$ are $x = -2$ and $x = 2$. Use the first derivative test to determine which of the critical values correspond to a local maximum.

4.  Given $f(x) = x + \dfrac{16}{x}$, $x < 0$, find the values of x corresponding to local maxima and local minima.

$$\left[ \text{NOTE: } f'(x) = \frac{x^2 - 16}{x^2} \right]$$

5.  Construct a sign chart for $f'(x)$ if $f(x) = -5 + \dfrac{3}{x} + \dfrac{4}{x^2}$.

6.  The cost of manufacturing x electric woks in one day is given by

$$C(x) = 8x^3 - 48x^2 + 6x$$

and the average cost per electric wok is given by

$$\overline{C}(x) = 8x^2 - 48x + 6.$$

Find the interval where the average cost per electric wok is decreasing.

7.  Find $f''(x)$ for $f(x) = -6x^8 - x^2$.

8.  Determine the intervals over which $f(x) = (x - 3)^3$ is concave downward.

9.  Find all inflection points for $f(x) = x^4 - 10x^3 + 24x^2 + 2x - 3$.

10. The critical values of $f(x)$ are $x = -5$ and $x = -3$. Use the sign chart for $f''(x)$ given below to find local maxima of $f(x)$.

$f''(x)$      $+ + + + 0 - - - -$
                            |              → x
                           -4

## CHAPTER 10   Additional Derivative Topics

11. Sketch the graph of f, a continuous function, using the information given below.

| x | f(x) | f'(x) | f''(x) |
|----|------|-------|--------|
| -1 | 0 | – | + |
| 1 | -4 | 0 | + |
| 3 | 0 | 4 | 0 |
| 5 | 4 | 0 | – |
| 7 | 0 | – | – |

f'(x):   – – – – 0 + + + + + + + 0 – – – –
                  |               |
                  1               5

f''(x):  + + + + + + + + 0 – – – – – – – – –
                         |
                         3

12. A company estimates that it will sell N(t) hair dryers after spending $t thousand on advertising, as given by:

    $N(t) = -t^3 + 165t^2 - 9,000t + 1,200$     $50 \leq t \leq 60$

    For which values of t is the rate of sales N'(t) increasing?

13. Sketch a graph of a function f with the following properties:

    f(1) = 8, f(3) = 8
    f is continuous for all x, except x = 2
    x = 2 is a vertical asymptote, y = 4 is a horizontal asymptote
    f'(x) > 0 for (-10, 2), f'(x) < 0 for (2, 10)
    f''(x) > 0 for (-10, 2) and for (2, 10)

14. Find horizontal asymptotes, if any, for $f(x) = \dfrac{5x^2 - 4}{7x + 3}$.

15. Find vertical asymptotes for $f(x) = \dfrac{4x - 2}{x^2 - 9}$.

16. Sketch a graph of $f(x) = \dfrac{1}{3}x^3 - x + 2$.

17. Sketch a graph of $f(x) = \dfrac{1}{4}x^4 - \dfrac{2}{3}x^3 + 2$.

18. Sketch a graph of $f(x) = \dfrac{2x - 2}{x + 2}$. Include any vertical or horizontal asymptotes.

## CHAPTER 10    Additional Derivative Topics

19. Given the total cost function $C(x) = 800 + \frac{1}{2}x^2$, graph the average

    cost function $\overline{C}(x)$ and the marginal cost function $C'(x)$ on the
    on the same set of axes.

20. Find the absolute maximum and minimum values of
    $f(x) = 6x^3 - 144x^2 + 1,134x - 12$ on the interval $[4, 8]$.

21. The average manufacturing cost per unit (in hundreds of dollars) for
    producing x units of a product is given by:

    $$\overline{C}(x) = 2x^3 - 48x^2 + 360x + 12 \qquad 1 \le x \le 5$$

    At what production level will the average cost per unit be maximum?

22. A drug that stimulates reproduction is introduced into a colony of
    bacteria. After t minutes, the number of bacteria is given
    approximately by:

    $$N(t) = 1,500 + 27t^2 - t^3 \qquad 0 \le t \le 30$$

    At what value of t is the rate of growth maximum?

23. A trailer rental agency rents 10 trailers per day at a rate of $30
    per day. For each $5 increase in rate, one less trailer is rented.
    At what rate should the trailers be rented to produce the maximum
    income? How many trailers will be rented?

24. A fence is to be erected to enclose a rectangular area adjacent to a
    building. The building, 60 feet long, will be used as part of the
    fencing on one side of the area (see figure below). Find the
    dimensions that will enclose the largest area if 300 feet of fencing
    material is used.

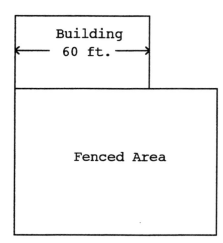

CHAPTER 10    Additional Derivative Topics

25. A company manufactures and sells x pocket calculators per week.
    If the weekly cost and demand equations are

    $C(x) = 5,000 + 5x$

    $p = 14 - \dfrac{x}{3,000}$      $0 \le x \le 25,000$

    find the production level that maximizes profit.

26. A computer software company sells 45,000 copies of a certain computer
    game each year. It costs the company $1.00 to store each copy of the
    game for one year. Each time it must produce additional copies, it
    costs the company $100 to set up production. How many copies of the
    game should the company produce during each production run in order
    to minimize its total storage and set-up costs?

27. A rancher wants to build a fence to enclose a 12,800 square yard
    rectangular field for cattle. The fence along one side is to be
    made of heavy-duty material that costs $15 per yard. The material
    along the remaining three sides costs only $5 per yard. Find the
    dimensions and total cost of fencing for the field that is least
    expensive to fence.

28. A 50 room hotel is filled to capacity every night at a rate of $150
    per room. The management wants to determine if a rate increase would
    increase their profit. They are not interested in a rate decrease.
    Suppose management determines that for each $3 increase in the
    nightly rate, five fewer rooms will be rented. If each rented room
    costs $15 a day to service, how much should the management charge
    per room to maximize profit?

29. Find x to two decimal places.

    (a) $x = 5,000e^{0.21}$
    (b) $8 = e^{0.24x}$

30. What amount (to the nearest cent) will an account have after 6 years
    if $100 is invested at 7.0% interest compounded continuously?

31. How long will it take for an account to have $910 if $250 is deposited
    at 13% interest compounded continuously?

32. An investor buys 100 shares of a stock for $25,000. After 4 years the
    stock is sold for $40,000. If interest is compounded continuously,
    what annual nominal rate of interest did the original $25,000
    investment earn? (Represent the answer as a percent to three decimal
    places.)

33. Radioactive carbon-14 has a continuous compound rate of decay of
    $r = -0.000124$. Estimate the age of a skull uncovered at an
    archaeological site if 14% of the original amount of carbon-14 is
    still present. (Compute answer to the nearest year.)

CHAPTER 10    Additional Derivative Topics

34. Find $D_x f(x)$ for $f(x) = 5e^x + 5 \ln(x^3)$.

35. Given $f(x) = 1 + e^x$, for what values of x is:
    (A) $f(x)$ increasing?
    (B) $f(x)$ decreasing?
    (C) the graph of f concave upward?
    (D) the graph of f concave downward?

36. Sketch the graph of $f(x) = 2 + e^x$.

37. Given $f(x) = -2 - \ln x$, for what values of x is:
    (A) $f(x)$ increasing?
    (B) $f(x)$ decreasing?
    (C) the graph of f concave upward?
    (D) the graph of f concave downward?

38. Sketch the graph of $f(x) = 3 + \ln x$.

39. The market research department of a national food company chose a
    large city in the Midwest to test market a new cereal.  They found
    that the weekly demand for the cereal is given approximately by

    $p = 10 - \ln x$

    where x is the number of boxes of cereal (in hundreds) sold each
    week and $p is the price of each box of cereal.  If each box of
    the cereal costs $0.85 for the company to produce, how should the
    cereal be priced in order to maximize the weekly profit?

40. Find $f'(x)$ for $f(x) = 3e^{8x} + 8 \ln(8x - 7)$.

41. Find $\frac{dy}{dx}$ given $y = \ln(4x^5 - x^2 + x)$.

42. Let $y = w^4$, $w = 4 + 2u$, $u = \ln x$.  Express y in terms of x and
    find $\frac{dx}{dy}$.

43. Find $D_x \left(5 + e^{3x^2+x}\right)^4$.

44. Find $f'(x)$ for $f(x) = 4^{3x+3}$.

45. Graph: $f(x) = 4 - 3e^{-2x}$

46. The salvage value S, in dollars, of a company's mainframe computer
    after t years is estimated to be given by:

    $S(t) = 500,000e^{-1.25t}$

    What is the rate of depreciation in dollars per year after 3 years?

CHAPTER 10    Additional Derivative Topics

47.  Suppose the price-demand equation for x units of a product is
     estimated to be $p = 90e^{-0.25x}$ where x units are sold per day at a
     price of p hundred dollars each.  Find the production level and price
     that maximize revenue.

Key Sheet - CHAPTER 10

[1]   $-3 \leq x \leq 2$

[2]   $\left[0,\ 3\right)$

[3]   $x = -2$

[4]   Local maximum: at $x = -4$
      (No local minimum for $x < 0$)

[5]
$$f'(x) \xrightarrow{\quad ----- 0 + + ND ----\quad} x$$
$$-\frac{8}{3} \qquad 0$$

[6]   The average cost is decreasing for $0 < x < 3$.

[7]   $f''(x) = -336x^6 - 2$

[8]   $(-\infty,\ 3)$

[9]   $x = 1$ and $x = 4$

[10]  $x = -3$

[11]
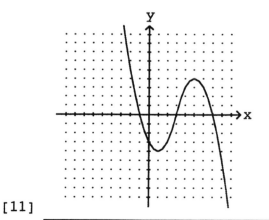

[12]  increasing on $50 < t < 55$

Key Sheet - CHAPTER 10

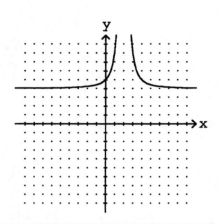

[13] _____

[14] No horizontal asymptote
_____

[15] x = -3, x = 3
_____

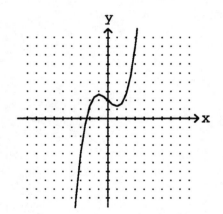

[16] _____

Key Sheet - CHAPTER 10

[17]
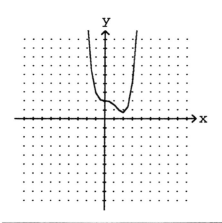

[18]
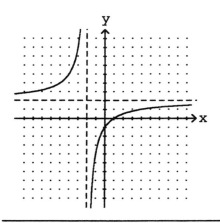

[19]
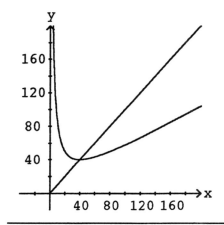

[20] Absolute minimum: f(4) = 2,604
Absolute maximum: f(7) = 2,928

Key Sheet - CHAPTER 10

[21] 5 units

[22] 9 minutes

[23] $40, 8 trailers

[24] 90 by 90 feet

[25] The maximum profit is realized when 13,500 pocket calculators are produced weekly.

[26] Costs will be minimized by producing 3,000 copies of the game 15 times during the year.

[27] The field should be 80 yd by 160 yd, with the shorter side using the more expensive fencing.  The cost of fencing should be $3,200.

[28] The management should leave the rate as it is.

[29] (a) 6,168.39
     (b) 8.66

[30] $152.20

[31] 9.94 years

[32] 11.750%

[33] 15,856 years

[34] $5e^x + \dfrac{15}{x}$

[35] (A) all x
     (B) none
     (C) all x
     (D) none

Key Sheet - CHAPTER 10

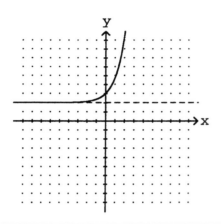

[36]

(A)  none
(B)  x > 0
(C)  x > 0
[37] (D)  none

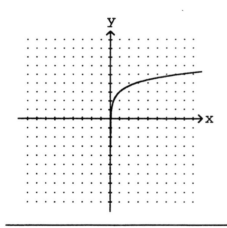

[38]

[39] $1.85

[40]  $f'(x) = 24e^{8x} + \dfrac{64}{8x - 7}$

[41]  $\dfrac{20x^4 - 2x + 1}{4x^5 - x^2 + x}$

[42]  $\dfrac{8(4 + 2 \ln x)^3}{x}$

## Key Sheet - CHAPTER 10

[43]  $4\left(5 + e^{3x^2+x}\right)^3 e^{3x^2+x}(6x + 1)$

[44]  $3\left(4^{3x+3}\right)(\ln 4)$

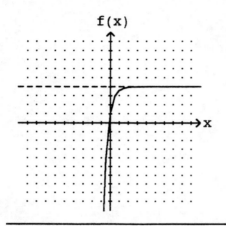

[45]

[46]  –$14,698.59

[47]  x = 4 units; p = $3,310.91

## CHAPTER 10    Additional Derivative Topics

1.  Solve the inequality: $x^2 + 2x - 8 \geq 0$

2.  Given $f(x) = 3x^3 - 9x^2 + 5$, for which values of x is $f(x)$ decreasing?

3.  The critical values of $f(x) = 2x^3 + 6x^2 - 18x + 6$ are x = -3 and x = 1. Use the first derivative test to determine which of the critical values correspond to a local minimum.

4.  Given $f(x) = x + \dfrac{36}{x}$, x > 0, find the values of x corresponding to local maxima and local minima.
    $$\left[ \text{NOTE: } f'(x) = \frac{x^2 - 36}{x^2} \right]$$

5.  Construct a sign chart for $f'(x)$ if $f(x) = 7 + \dfrac{8}{x} + \dfrac{1}{x^2}$.

6.  The cost of manufacturing x electric woks in one day is given by
    $$C(x) = 2x^3 - 28x^2 + 5x$$
    and the average cost per electric wok is given by
    $$\overline{C}(x) = 2x^2 - 28x + 5.$$
    Find the interval where the average cost per electric wok is decreasing.

7.  Find $f''(x)$ for $f(x) = -x^4 - 9x^2$.

8.  Determine the intervals over which $f(x) = (x - 3)^3$ is concave upward.

9.  Find all inflection points for $f(x) = x^4 - 14x^3 + 72x^2 + x + 5$.

10. The critical values of $f(x)$ are x = -7 and x = -3. Use the sign chart for $f''(x)$ given below to find local minima of $f(x)$.

    $f''(x)$      – – – – 0 + + + +
                  _____|_____→ x
                         -5

CHAPTER 10    Additional Derivative Topics

11.  Sketch the graph of f, a continuous function, using the information
     given below.

| x | f(x) | f'(x) | f''(x) |
|----|------|-------|--------|
| -3 | 0 | + | - |
| -1 | 4 | 0 | - |
| 1 | 0 | -4 | 0 |
| 3 | -4 | 0 | + |
| 5 | 0 | + | + |

f'(x):  + + + + 0 - - - - - - - 0 + + + +

                    -1              3

f''(x):  - - - - - - - - 0 + + + + + + + + +

                        1

12.  A company estimates that it will sell N(t) hair dryers after spending
     $t thousand on advertising, as given by:

     $N(t) = -t^3 + 120t^2 - 3,600t + 1,050 \qquad 20 \leq t \leq 60$

     For which values of t is the rate of sales N'(t) increasing?

13.  Sketch a graph of a function f with the following properties:

     $f(3) = 4$, $f(5) = 4$
     f is continuous for all x, except $x = 4$
     $x = 4$ is a vertical asymptote, $y = 3$ is a horizontal asymptote
     $f'(x) > 0$ for $(-10, 4)$, $f'(x) < 0$ for $(4, 10)$
     $f''(x) > 0$ for $(-10, 4)$ and for $(4, 10)$

14.  Find horizontal asymptotes, if any, for $f(x) = \dfrac{3x^2}{2x - 1}$.

15.  Find vertical asymptotes for $f(x) = \dfrac{6x + 2}{x^2 - 5x + 6}$.

16.  Sketch a graph of $f(x) = -\dfrac{1}{3}x^3 + \dfrac{1}{2}x^2 + 2x - 3$.

17.  Sketch a graph of $f(x) = \dfrac{1}{4}x^4 - x^3 + 1$.

18.  Sketch a graph of $f(x) = \dfrac{-2x + 2}{x - 3}$.  Include any vertical or horizontal
     asymptotes.

## CHAPTER 10    Additional Derivative Topics

19. Given the total cost function $C(x) = 900 + \frac{1}{4}x^2$, graph the average

    cost function $\overline{C}(x)$ and the marginal cost function $C'(x)$ on the
    on the same set of axes.

20. Find the absolute maximum and minimum values of
    $f(x) = 7x^3 - 105x^2 + 441x + 5$ on the interval [6, 9].

21. The average manufacturing cost per unit (in hundreds of dollars) for
    producing x units of a product is given by:

    $\overline{C}(x) = 2x^3 - 48x^2 + 360x + 10 \qquad 6 \leq x \leq 9$

    At what production level will the average cost per unit be minimum?

22. A drug that stimulates reproduction is introduced into a colony of
    bacteria. After t minutes, the number of bacteria is given
    approximately by:

    $N(t) = 2,000 + 24t^2 - t^3 \qquad 0 \leq t \leq 30$

    At what value of t is the rate of growth maximum?

23. A trailer rental agency rents 12 trailers per day at a rate of $24
    per day. For each $4 increase in rate, one less trailer is rented.
    At what rate should the trailers be rented to produce the maximum
    income? How many trailers will be rented?

24. A fence is to be erected to enclose a rectangular area adjacent to a
    building. The building, 72 feet long, will be used as part of the
    fencing on one side of the area (see figure below). Find the
    dimensions that will enclose the largest area if 360 feet of fencing
    material is used.

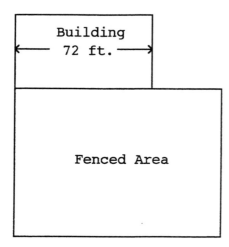

CHAPTER 10    Additional Derivative Topics

25.  A company manufactures and sells x pocket calculators per week.
     If the weekly cost and demand equations are

     $C(x) = 9{,}000 + 6x$

     $p = 12 - \dfrac{x}{6{,}000}$     $0 \le x \le 25{,}000$

     find the production level that maximizes profit.

26.  A computer software company sells 125,000 copies of a certain computer
     game each year.  It costs the company $0.20 to store each copy of the
     game for one year.  Each time it must produce additional copies, it
     costs the company $125 to set up production.  How many copies of the
     game should the company produce during each production run in order
     to minimize its total storage and set-up costs?

27.  A rancher wants to build a fence to enclose a 5,000 square yard
     rectangular field for cattle.  The fence along one side is to be
     made of heavy-duty material that costs $27 per yard.  The material
     along the remaining three sides costs only $9 per yard.  Find the
     dimensions and total cost of fencing for the field that is least
     expensive to fence.

28.  An 80 room hotel is filled to capacity every night at a rate of $100
     per room.  The management wants to determine if a rate increase would
     increase their profit.  They are not interested in a rate decrease.
     Suppose management determines that for each $4 increase in the
     nightly rate, five fewer rooms will be rented.  If each rented room
     costs $16 a day to service, how much should the management charge
     per room to maximize profit?

29.  Find x to two decimal places.

     (a) $x = 9{,}000e^{0.06}$
     (b) $8 = e^{0.20x}$

30.  What amount (to the nearest cent) will an account have after 5 years
     if $175 is invested at 8.0% interest compounded continuously?

31.  How long will it take for an account to have $890 if $400 is deposited
     at 11% interest compounded continuously?

32.  An investor buys 100 shares of a stock for $15,000.  After 6 years the
     stock is sold for $24,000.  If interest is compounded continuously,
     what annual nominal rate of interest did the original $15,000
     investment earn?  (Represent the answer as a percent to three decimal
     places.)

33.  Radioactive carbon-14 has a continuous compound rate of decay of
     $r = -0.000124$.  Estimate the age of a skull uncovered at an
     archaeological site if 13% of the original amount of carbon-14 is
     still present.  (Compute answer to the nearest year.)

CHAPTER 10    Additional Derivative Topics

34.  Find $D_x f(x)$ for $f(x) = 7e^x + 3 \ln(x^4)$.

35.  Given $f(x) = 2 - e^x$, for what values of x is:
     (A) $f(x)$ increasing?
     (B) $f(x)$ decreasing?
     (C) the graph of f concave upward?
     (D) the graph of f concave downward?

36.  Sketch the graph of $f(x) = -1 + e^x$.

37.  Given $f(x) = 1 + \ln x$, for what values of x is:
     (A) $f(x)$ increasing?
     (B) $f(x)$ decreasing?
     (C) the graph of f concave upward?
     (D) the graph of f concave downward?

38.  Sketch the graph of $f(x) = 3 + \ln x$.

39.  The market research department of a national food company chose a
     large city in the Midwest to test market a new cereal.  They found
     that the weekly demand for the cereal is given approximately by

     $p = 8 - 2 \ln x$

     where x is the number of boxes of cereal (in hundreds) sold each
     week and $p is the price of each box of cereal.  If each box of
     the cereal costs $1.20 for the company to produce, how should the
     cereal be priced in order to maximize the weekly profit?

40.  Find $f'(x)$ for $f(x) = 7e^{2x} + 7 \ln(2x - 7)$.

41.  Find $\frac{dy}{dx}$ given $y = \ln(3x^5 + x^2 - x)$.

42.  Let $y = w^2$, $w = 3 - 2u$, $u = \ln x$.  Express y in terms of x and
     find $\frac{dx}{dy}$.

43.  Find $D_x \left(1 + e^{2x^2 + 4x}\right)^2$.

44.  Find $f'(x)$ for $f(x) = 2^{2x+2}$.

45.  Graph: $f(x) = -2 - e^{-3x}$

46.  The salvage value S, in dollars, of a company's mainframe computer
     after t years is estimated to be given by:

     $S(t) = 900,000e^{-0.30t}$

     What is the rate of depreciation in dollars per year after 2 years?

CHAPTER 10    Additional Derivative Topics

47.    Suppose the price-demand equation for x units of a product is
estimated to be $p = 90e^{-0.25x}$ where x units are sold per day at a
price of p hundred dollars each.  Find the production level and price
that maximize revenue.

Key Sheet - CHAPTER 10

[1]  $x \leq -4$ or $x \geq 2$

[2]  $(0, 2]$

[3]  $x = 1$

[4]  Local minimum: at $x = 6$
     (No local maximum for $x > 0$)

[5]
$$
\begin{array}{c}
\quad\quad - - - - - 0 + + \text{ND} - - - - \\
f'(x) \underline{\hspace{3cm}} \rightarrow x \\
\quad\quad\quad -\frac{1}{4} \quad\quad 0
\end{array}
$$

[6]  The average cost is decreasing for $0 < x < 7$.

[7]  $f''(x) = -12x^2 - 18$

[8]  $(3, \infty)$

[9]  $x = 3$ and $x = 4$

[10]  $x = -3$

[11]
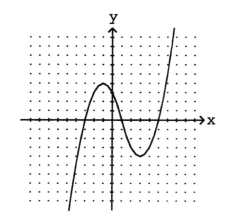

[12]  increasing on $20 < t < 40$

Key Sheet - CHAPTER 10

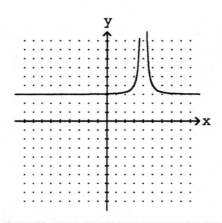

[13] _____

[14] No horizontal asymptote

[15] x = 3,  x = 2

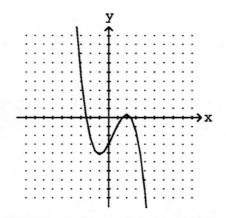

[16] _____

Key Sheet - CHAPTER 10

[17]

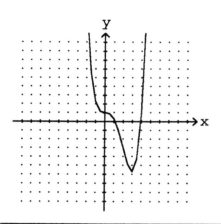

[18]

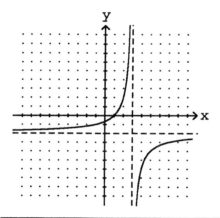

[19]

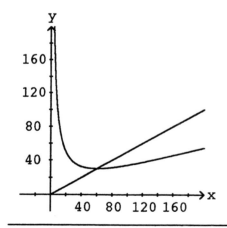

[20] Absolute minimum: f(7) = 348
Absolute maximum: f(9) = 572

## Key Sheet – CHAPTER 10

[21] 9 units

[22] 8 minutes

[23] $36, 9 trailers

[24] 108 by 108 feet

[25] The maximum profit is realized when 18,000 pocket calculators are produced weekly.

[26] Costs will be minimized by producing 12,500 copies of the game 10 times during the year.

[27] The field should be 50 yd by 100 yd, with the shorter side using the more expensive fencing. The cost of fencing should be $3,600.

[28] The management should leave the rate as it is.

[29] (a) 9,556.53
     (b) 10.40

[30] $261.07

[31] 7.27 years

[32] 7.833%

[33] 16,453 years

[34] $7e^x + \dfrac{12}{x}$

[35] (A) none
     (B) all x
     (C) none
     (D) all x

## Key Sheet - CHAPTER 10

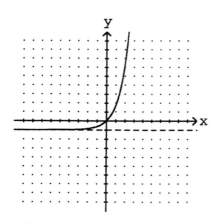

[36]

(A)  x > 0
(B)  none
(C)  none
[37]  (D)  x > 0

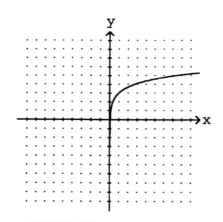

[38]

[39]  $3.20

[40]  $f'(x) = 14e^{2x} + \dfrac{14}{2x - 7}$

[41]  $\dfrac{15x^4 + 2x - 1}{3x^5 + x^2 - x}$

[42]  $\dfrac{-4(3 - 2 \ln x)}{x}$

[43] $2\left(1 + e^{2x^2+4x}\right)e^{2x^2+4x}(4x + 4)$

[44] $2\left(2^{2x+2}\right)(\ln 2)$

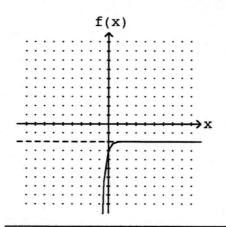

[45]

[46] -$148,179.14

[47] $x = 4$ units; $p = \$3,310.91$

# DellenTest MAC 2.0

Copyright © 1995 by Prentice-Hall, Inc.

Essentials of College Mathematics, Third Edition
Raymond A. Barnett and Michael R. Ziegler

Form A-C

Page 1

## CHAPTER 10   Additional Derivative Topics

1. Solve the inequality: $x^2 - 3x + 2 \geq 0$

2. Given $f(x) = 2x^3 - 18x^2 - 4$, for which values of x is $f(x)$ decreasing?

3. The critical values of $f(x) = -4x^3 + 6x^2 + 72x - 36$ are $x = -2$ and $x = 3$. Use the first derivative test to determine which of the critical values correspond to a local minimum.

4. Given $f(x) = x + \dfrac{1}{x}$, $x < 0$, find the values of x corresponding to local maxima and local minima.
$$\left[ \text{NOTE: } f'(x) = \frac{x^2 - 1}{x^2} \right]$$

5. Construct a sign chart for $f'(x)$ if $f(x) = -4 + \dfrac{3}{x} + \dfrac{8}{x^2}$.

6. The cost of manufacturing x electric woks in one day is given by
$$C(x) = 8x^3 - 112x^2 + 11x$$
and the average cost per electric wok is given by
$$\overline{C}(x) = 8x^2 - 112x + 11.$$
Find the interval where the average cost per electric wok is decreasing.

7. Find $f''(x)$ for $f(x) = 7x^4 + 7x^2$.

8. Determine the intervals over which $f(x) = (x - 2)^3$ is concave upward.

9. Find all inflection points for $f(x) = x^4 - 8x^3 + 18x^2 - x + 1$.

10. The critical values of $f(x)$ are $x = -7$ and $x = -1$. Use the sign chart for $f''(x)$ given below to find local minima of $f(x)$.

$f''(x)$      + + + + 0 - - - -

$\xrightarrow{\hspace{3cm}}$ x

$\qquad\quad -4$

CHAPTER 10     Additional Derivative Topics

11.  Sketch the graph of f, a continuous function, using the information
     given below.

| x | f(x) | f'(x) | f''(x) |
|---|------|-------|--------|
| -3 | 0 | − | + |
| -1 | -4 | 0 | + |
| 1 | 0 | 4 | 0 |
| 3 | 4 | 0 | − |
| 5 | 0 | − | − |

f'(x):   − − − − 0 + + + + + + + 0 − − − −
                   |                 |
                  −1                 3

f''(x):  + + + + + + + + 0 − − − − − − − −
                         |
                         1

12.  A company estimates that it will sell N(t) hair dryers after spending
     $t thousand on advertising, as given by:

     $$N(t) = -2t^3 + 330t^2 - 18,000t + 1,650 \qquad 50 \le t \le 60$$

     For which values of t is the rate of sales N'(t) increasing?

13.  Sketch a graph of a function f with the following properties:

     $f(1) = 7$, $f(3) = 7$
     f is continuous for all x, except $x = 2$
     $x = 2$ is a vertical asymptote, $y = 4$ is a horizontal asymptote
     $f'(x) > 0$ for $(-10, 2)$, $f'(x) < 0$ for $(2, 10)$
     $f''(x) > 0$ for $(-10, 2)$ and for $(2, 10)$

14.  Find horizontal asymptotes, if any, for $f(x) = \dfrac{8x + 3}{6x^3 - 4}$.

15.  Find vertical asymptotes for $f(x) = \dfrac{7x + 2}{x^2 + x - 6}$.

16.  Sketch a graph of $f(x) = \frac{1}{3}x^3 - 2x^2 + 3x + 2$.

17.  Sketch a graph of $f(x) = \frac{1}{4}x^4 - x^3 + 3$.

18.  Sketch a graph of $f(x) = \dfrac{3x - 1}{x - 1}$.  Include any vertical or horizontal
     asymptotes.

---

CHAPTER 10     Additional Derivative Topics

---

19. Given the total cost function $C(x) = 2,700 + \frac{1}{3}x^2$, graph the average
    cost function $\overline{C}(x)$ and the marginal cost function $C'(x)$ on the
    on the same set of axes.

20. Find the absolute maximum and minimum values of
    $f(x) = 5x^3 + 15x^2 - 525x + 3$ on the interval $[4, 6]$.

21. The average manufacturing cost per unit (in hundreds of dollars) for
    producing x units of a product is given by:

    $\overline{C}(x) = 2x^3 - 48x^2 + 360x + 12 \qquad 1 \le x \le 5$

    At what production level will the average cost per unit be maximum?

22. A drug that stimulates reproduction is introduced into a colony of
    bacteria. After t minutes, the number of bacteria is given
    approximately by:

    $N(t) = 1,000 + 33t^2 - t^3 \qquad 0 \le t \le 30$

    At what value of t is the rate of growth maximum?

23. A trailer rental agency rents 12 trailers per day at a rate of $18
    per day. For each $3 increase in rate, one less trailer is rented.
    At what rate should the trailers be rented to produce the maximum
    income? How many trailers will be rented?

24. A fence is to be erected to enclose a rectangular area adjacent to a
    building. The building, 72 feet long, will be used as part of the
    fencing on one side of the area (see figure below). Find the
    dimensions that will enclose the largest area if 300 feet of fencing
    material is used.

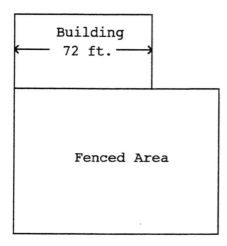

## CHAPTER 10    Additional Derivative Topics

25. A company manufactures and sells x pocket calculators per week. If the weekly cost and demand equations are

    $C(x) = 4,000 + 5x$

    $p = 14 - \dfrac{x}{4,000}$     $0 \le x \le 25,000$

    find the production level that maximizes profit.

26. A computer software company sells 20,000 copies of a certain computer game each year. It costs the company $0.60 to store each copy of the game for one year. Each time it must produce additional copies, it costs the company $375 to set up production. How many copies of the game should the company produce during each production run in order to minimize its total storage and set-up costs?

27. A rancher wants to build a fence to enclose a 9,800 square yard rectangular field for cattle. The fence along one side is to be made of heavy-duty material that costs $18 per yard. The material along the remaining three sides costs only $6 per yard. Find the dimensions and total cost of fencing for the field that is least expensive to fence.

28. A 90 room hotel is filled to capacity every night at a rate of $50 per room. The management wants to determine if a rate increase would increase their profit. They are not interested in a rate decrease. Suppose management determines that for each $2 increase in the nightly rate, five fewer rooms will be rented. If each rented room costs $8 a day to service, how much should the management charge per room to maximize profit?

29. Find x to two decimal places.

    (a) $x = 5,000e^{0.22}$
    (b) $8 = e^{0.13x}$

30. What amount (to the nearest cent) will an account have after 9 years if $125 is invested at 8.0% interest compounded continuously?

31. How long will it take for an account to have $860 if $300 is deposited at 13% interest compounded continuously?

32. An investor buys 100 shares of a stock for $10,000. After 5 years the stock is sold for $16,000. If interest is compounded continuously, what annual nominal rate of interest did the original $10,000 investment earn? (Represent the answer as a percent to three decimal places.)

33. Radioactive carbon-14 has a continuous compound rate of decay of $r = -0.000124$. Estimate the age of a skull uncovered at an archaeological site if 11% of the original amount of carbon-14 is still present. (Compute answer to the nearest year.)

CHAPTER 10    Additional Derivative Topics

34. Find $D_x f(x)$ for $f(x) = 8e^x - 2 \ln(x^3)$.

35. Given $f(x) = 3 - e^x$, for what values of x is:
   (A) $f(x)$ increasing?
   (B) $f(x)$ decreasing?
   (C) the graph of f concave upward?
   (D) the graph of f concave downward?

36. Sketch the graph of $f(x) = 3 - e^x$.

37. Given $f(x) = 1 + \ln x$, for what values of x is:
   (A) $f(x)$ increasing?
   (B) $f(x)$ decreasing?
   (C) the graph of f concave upward?
   (D) the graph of f concave downward?

38. Sketch the graph of $f(x) = 1 + \ln x$.

39. The market research department of a national food company chose a
    large city in the Midwest to test market a new cereal. They found
    that the weekly demand for the cereal is given approximately by

    $p = 5 - \ln x$

    where x is the number of boxes of cereal (in hundreds) sold each
    week and $p is the price of each box of cereal. If each box of
    the cereal costs $1.35 for the company to produce, how should the
    cereal be priced in order to maximize the weekly profit?

40. Find $f'(x)$ for $f(x) = 9e^{2x} - 4 \ln(6x + 1)$.

41. Find $\frac{dy}{dx}$ given $y = \ln(2x^5 - x^3 - 4x)$.

42. Let $y = w^2$, $w = 4 + 3u$, $u = \ln x$. Express y in terms of x and
    find $\frac{dx}{dy}$.

43. Find $D_x \left(3 + e^{5x^2+x}\right)^4$.

44. Find $f'(x)$ for $f(x) = 5^{2x+4}$.

45. Graph: $f(x) = 3 - 2e^{3x}$

46. The salvage value S, in dollars, of a company's mainframe computer
    after t years is estimated to be given by:

    $S(t) = 700,000e^{-0.05t}$

    What is the rate of depreciation in dollars per year after 8 years?

CHAPTER 10    Additional Derivative Topics

47.   Suppose the price-demand equation for x units of a product is estimated to be $p = 30e^{-0.10x}$ where x units are sold per day at a price of p hundred dollars each.  Find the production level and price that maximize revenue.

Key Sheet - CHAPTER 10

[1]  x ≤ 1 or x ≥ 2

[2]  $(0, 6]$

[3]  x = -2

[4]  Local maximum: at x = -1
     (No local minimum for x < 0)

[5]
$$f'(x) \quad \underset{-\frac{16}{3} \qquad 0}{\underline{\quad - - - - - \; 0 \; + \; + \; ND \; - - - - - \quad}} \longrightarrow x$$

[6]  The average cost is decreasing for 0 < x < 7.

[7]  $f''(x) = 84x^2 + 14$

[8]  (2, ∞)

[9]  x = 1 and x = 3

[10] x = -7

[11]
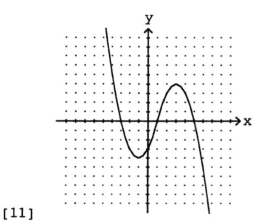

[12] increasing on 50 < t < 55

Key Sheet - CHAPTER 10

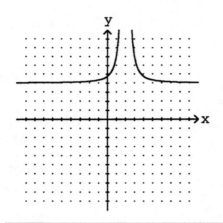

[13] _____

[14] y = 0

[15] x = -3, x = 2

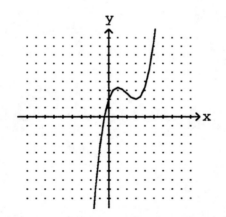

[16] _____

[17]

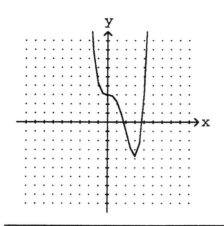

[18]

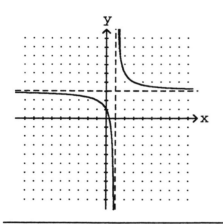

[19]

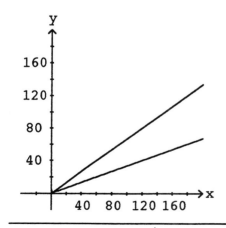

[20] Absolute minimum: f(5) = -1,622
Absolute maximum: f(6) = -1,527

## Key Sheet - CHAPTER 10

[21] 5 units

[22] 11 minutes

[23] $27, 9 trailers

[24] 93 by 93 feet

[25] The maximum profit is realized when 18,000 pocket calculators are produced weekly.

[26] Costs will be minimized by producing 5,000 copies of the game 4 times during the year.

[27] The field should be 70 yd by 140 yd, with the shorter side using the more expensive fencing.  The cost of fencing should be $3,360.

[28] The management should leave the rate as it is.

[29] (a) 6,230.38
(b) 16.00

[30] $256.80

[31] 8.10 years

[32] 9.400%

[33] 17,801 years

[34] $8e^x - \dfrac{6}{x}$

[35] (A) none
(B) all x
(C) none
(D) all x

Key Sheet - CHAPTER 10

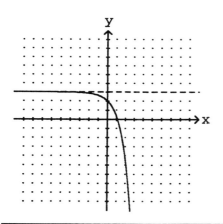

[36]

(A)  x > 0
(B)  none
(C)  none
[37] (D)  x > 0

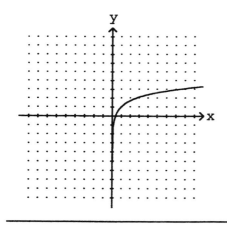

[38]

[39]  $2.35

[40]  $f'(x) = 18e^{2x} + \dfrac{-24}{6x + 1}$

[41]  $\dfrac{10x^4 - 3x^2 - 4}{2x^5 - x^3 - 4x}$

[42]  $\dfrac{6(4 + 3 \ln x)}{x}$

[43] $4\left(3 + e^{5x^2+x}\right)^3 e^{5x^2+x}(10x + 1)$

[44] $2\left(5^{2x+4}\right)(\ln 5)$

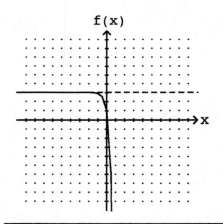

[45]

[46] –$23,461.20

[47] x = 10 units; p = $1,103.64

Essentials of College Mathematics, Third Edition
Raymond A. Barnett and Michael R. Ziegler

## CHAPTER 11    Integration

1. Find: $\int \left(x^5 + 5x^3 + 4\right) dx$

2. Find: $\int \left(2x^{5/7} + \dfrac{3}{x^4}\right) dx$

3. Find: $\int \left(\dfrac{7}{\sqrt[3]{x^2}} + 8\sqrt{x}\right) dx$

4. Find: $\int \left(-e^x - \dfrac{2}{x}\right) dx$

5. Find $f(x)$ if $f'(x) = \dfrac{-1}{x^3}$ and $f(1) = 1$.

6. If the marginal profit for producing x units is given by

   $P'(x) = 50 - 0.18x \qquad P(0) = -200$

   where $P(x)$ is profit in dollars, find the profit function P and the profit on 100 units.

7. A newspaper is launching a new advertising campaign in order to increase the number of daily subscribers. The newspaper currently (t = 0) has 26,000 daily subscribers and management expects that number, $S(t)$, to grow at the rate of

   $S'(t) = 60t^{1/2}$

   subscribers per day, where t is the number of days since the campaign began. How long should the campaign last if the newspaper wants the number of daily subscribers to grow to 41,000?

8. The marginal revenue from the sale of compact discs is given by

   $R'(x) = 110 - 16x \qquad R(0) = 0$

   where $R(x)$ is the revenue in dollars. Find the price-demand equation.

9. Find: $\int \left(6x^6 - 5\right)^2 x^5 \, dx$

10. Find: $\int \dfrac{x}{(2x^2 + 5)^6} \, dx$

## CHAPTER 11    Integration

11.  Find: $\displaystyle\int \frac{2x + 1}{2x^2 + 2x + 1}\, dx$

12.  Find: $\displaystyle\int (3 + 5x)e^{6x+5x^2}\, dx$

13.  Find: $\displaystyle\int x\sqrt{x + 7}\, dx$

14.  The marginal price for a weekly demand of x bottles of cough medicine in a drugstore is given by:

$$p'(x) = \frac{-41,200}{(8x + 30)^2}$$

Find the price-demand equation if the weekly demand is 125 when the price of a bottle of cough medicine is $5.  What is the weekly demand when the price is $3.25?

15.  A manufacturing company is ready to introduce a new product with a national sales campaign.  After extensive test marketing, the market research department estimates that sales (in millions of dollars) will increase at the monthly rate of

$$S'(t) = 7 - 7e^{-0.2t} \qquad 0 \le t \le 24$$

t months after the national campaign has started.  What will be the total sales 10 months after the beginning of the campaign if we assume zero sales at the beginning of the campaign?  (Round answer to the nearest million.)

16.  The management of an oil company estimates that oil will be pumped from a producing field at a rate given by

$$R(t) = \frac{52}{\sqrt{t + 8}} \qquad 0 \le t \le 20$$

where R(t) is the rate of production in thousands of barrels per year, t years after pumping begins.  How many barrels of oil, Q(t), will be produced the first 5 years?

17.  If the marginal price dp/dx at x units of demand per week is proportional to the price p, and if at $90 there is no weekly demand [p(0) = 90], and if at $60.18 there is a weekly demand of 9 units [p(9) = 60.18], find the price-demand equation.

18.  Given $\displaystyle\int_1^3 f(x)\,dx = 5$ and $\displaystyle\int_1^3 g(x)\,dx = 7$, use properties of definite integrals to evaluate $\displaystyle\int_1^3 [3f(x) + 2g(x)]\,dx$.

19.  Evaluate: $\displaystyle\int_{-2}^{1} \left(4x^3 - 4x\right)dx$

## CHAPTER 11    Integration

20. Evaluate: $\int_1^5 \left(-2\sqrt{x} - \frac{5}{x}\right) dx$

21. Evaluate: $\int_{0.1}^{0.3} 7e^{2x}\, dx$

22. Evaluate: $\int_0^2 \frac{6x^2 + 1}{8x^3 + 4x + 2}\, dx$

23. Evaluate: $\int_{-3}^0 \frac{x}{\sqrt{x + 4}}\, dx$

24. A factory discharges pollutants into a large river at a rate that is estimated by a water quality control agency to be

    $$P'(t) = t^2\sqrt{1 + t^3} \qquad 0 \le t \le 5$$

    where $P(t)$ is the total number of tons of pollutants discharged into the river after t years of operation. What quantity of pollutants will be discharged into the river from the end of the 3rd year to the end of the 4th year?

25. Test marketing for a new health-food snack product in a selected area suggests that sales (in thousands of dollars) will increase at a rate given by

    $$S'(t) = 10 - 10e^{-0.22t}$$

    t months after an aggressive national advertising campaign is begun. Find total sales during the second twelve months of the campaign.

26. A photocopy shop rents the use of a personal computer and accompanying software to the public. The total accumulated costs $C(t)$ and revenues $R(t)$ (in thousands of dollars) generated by the computer satisfy

    $$C'(t) = 1 \quad \text{and} \quad R'(t) = 16e^{-0.4t}$$

    where t is time in years. Find the useful life of the computer to the nearest tenth of a year, and calculate the total accumulated profit during the computer's useful life.

27. Find the area between the graph of $f(x) = e^{0.2x}$ and the x-axis over the interval $0 \le x \le 5$.

28. Find the area bounded by:

    $f(x) = x^2 - x - 12$ and $y = 0$ for $1 \le x \le 3$

29. Find the area between the graph of $f(x) = 243 - 3x^2$ and the x-axis over the interval $[-9, 9]$.

## CHAPTER 11    Integration

30. Find the area bounded by:

    $f(x) = 3 + 2x - x^2$ and $y = x + 1$

31. Find the area between the graph of $f(x) = x^2 - 4x$ and the x-axis over the interval $-2 \leq x \leq 3$.

32. The income distribution for a certain country is represented by the Lorenz curve with equation: $f(x) = \frac{4}{5}x^2 + \frac{1}{5}x$

    (A) Find the coefficient of inequality.
    (B) Use the answer found in (A) to determine if the income of this country is (more equally distributed, less equally distributed, distributed the same) as a second country having a coefficient of inequality of 0.2.

33. Use the rectangle rule to approximate $\int_1^9 \left(4 + x^3\right) dx$ using n = 4, and $c_k$ as the midpoint of each subinterval. Compute the approximation to three decimal places.

34. Use the table of values below and a Riemann Sum to approximate the definite integral. Use n = 4 and choose $c_k$ as the midpoint of each interval.

    $\int_4^{12} f(x) dx$

    | x    | 5  | 7  | 9  | 11 |
    |------|----|----|----|----|
    | f(x) | 40 | 96 | 26 | 67 |

35. The number of cheeseburgers (in thousands) sold each day by a chain of restaurants t days after the beginning of an advertising campaign is given by $S(t) = 9 - 8e^{-0.1t}$. What is the average number of cheeseburgers sold each day during the second seven days of the advertising campaign?

CHAPTER 11    Integration

36.  Let $R(t)$ and $C(t)$ represent the total accumulated revenues and costs
     (in dollars), respectively, for an oil well where t is time in years.
     The derivatives of R and C over a 4-year period are shown in the
     graph below.  Use the rectangle rule with n = 4 and $c_k$ as the midpoint
     of each subinterval to approximate the total accumulated profits from
     the well over this 4-year period.  Estimate necessary function values
     from the graph.

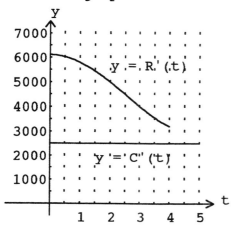

37.  A drug is injected into the bloodstream of a patient through her
     right arm.  The concentration of the drug, $C(t)$ (in milligrams per
     cubic centimeter), in the bloodstream of the left arm t hours after
     the injection is given by:

$$C(t) = \frac{0.19t}{t^2 + 5}$$

     What is the average concentration of the drug in the bloodstream of
     the left arm during the first 2 hours after the injection?

38.  Find the consumers' surplus at a price level of $8 for the
     price-demand equation:

$$p = D(x) = 22 - \frac{1}{20}x$$

39.  Find the producers' surplus at a price level of $9 for the
     price-supply equation:

$$p = S(x) = 5 + \frac{1}{100}x^2$$

40.  Find the equilibrium price if the price-demand equation is
     $p = D(x) = \frac{61}{3} - \frac{1}{20}x$, and the price-supply equation is
     $p = S(x) = 7 + \frac{1}{12,000}x^2$.

CHAPTER 11     Integration

41.  Find the equilibrium price, and then find the consumers' surplus and
     producers' surplus for:

$$p = D(x) = 67 - \frac{1}{10}x \quad \text{and} \quad p = S(x) = 31 + \frac{1}{20}x$$

Key Sheet - CHAPTER 11

[1]  $\frac{1}{6}x^6 + \frac{5}{4}x^4 + 4x + C$

[2]  $\frac{7}{6}x^{12/7} - \frac{1}{x^3} + C$

[3]  $21\sqrt[3]{x} + \frac{16}{3}\sqrt{x^3} + C$

[4]  $-e^x - 2\ln|x| + C$

[5]  $f(x) = \frac{1}{2}x^{-2} + \frac{1}{2}$

[6]  $P(x) = 50x - 0.09x^2 - 200$
     $P(100) = \$3,900$

[7]  The advertising campaign should last approximately 52 days.

[8]  $p = 110 - 8x$

[9]  $\frac{1}{108}\left(6x^6 - 5\right)^3 + C$

[10] $-\frac{1}{20}\left(2x^2 + 5\right)^{-5} + C$
     or $\frac{-1}{20\left(2x^2 + 5\right)^5} + C$

[11] $\frac{1}{2}\ln|2x^2 + 2x + 1| + C$

[12] $\frac{1}{2}e^{6x+5x^2} + C$

[13] $\frac{2}{5}(x + 7)^{5/2} - \frac{14}{3}(x + 7)^{3/2} + C$

[14] $p(x) = \frac{5,150}{8x + 30}$; the weekly demand is about 194 bottles when the price is $3.25.

[15] about $40 million

[16] About 81 thousand barrels will be produced.

[17] $p(x) = 90e^{-0.04x}$

[18] 29

[19] -9

[20] $-\frac{4}{3}\left(5^{3/2}\right) + 5 \ln 5 + \frac{4}{3} \approx -21.621$

[21] $\frac{7}{2}\left(e^{0.6} - e^{0.2}\right) \approx 2.103$

[22] $\frac{1}{4}(\ln 74 - \ln 2) \approx 0.903$

[23] $-\frac{10}{3}$

[24] $\frac{2}{9}(65^{3/2} - 28^{3/2})$ tons $\approx 83.53$ tons

[25] 116.99 thousand dollars

[26] useful life: 6.9 years
total profit: 30.6 thousand dollars

[27] 8.591

[28] $\frac{58}{3} \approx 19.33$

[29] 2,916

[30] $\frac{9}{2} = 4.50$

[31] $\frac{59}{3} \approx 19.67$

[32] (A) 0.27
(B) less equally distributed

[33] 1,632

[34] $\int_{4}^{12} f(x)dx \approx 458$

[35] 6.14 thousand cheeseburgers

[36] $9,500

[37] 0.028 mg

Key Sheet - CHAPTER 11

[38] $1,960

[39] $53.33

[40] $10.33

[41] $\bar{p}$ = 43; CS = $2,880; PS = $1,440

## DellenTest MAC 2.0
Copyright © 1995 by Prentice-Hall, Inc.

Essentials of College Mathematics, Third Edition
Raymond A. Barnett and Michael R. Ziegler

Form A-B

Page 1

## CHAPTER 11    Integration

1.   Find: $\int \left(7x^4 + 4x^3 - 1\right) dx$

2.   Find: $\int \left(-3x^{5/7} + \dfrac{2}{x^5}\right) dx$

3.   Find: $\int \left(\dfrac{-3}{\sqrt{x}} - 4\sqrt[3]{x}\right) dx$

4.   Find: $\int \left(2e^x + \dfrac{4}{x}\right) dx$

5.   Find $f(x)$ if $f'(x) = \dfrac{8}{x^4}$ and $f(1) = -2$.

6.   If the marginal profit for producing x units is given by

   $P'(x) = 80 - 0.16x \qquad P(0) = -300$

   where $P(x)$ is profit in dollars, find the profit function P and the profit on 200 units.

7.   A newspaper is launching a new advertising campaign in order to increase the number of daily subscribers.  The newspaper currently (t = 0) has 25,000 daily subscribers and management expects that number, S(t), to grow at the rate of

   $S'(t) = 50t^{4/5}$

   subscribers per day, where t is the number of days since the campaign began.  How long should the campaign last if the newspaper wants the number of daily subscribers to grow to 44,000?

8.   The marginal revenue from the sale of compact discs is given by

   $R'(x) = 130 - 6x \qquad R(0) = 0$

   where $R(x)$ is the revenue in dollars.  Find the price-demand equation.

9.   Find: $\int \left(4x^7 + 3\right)^3 x^6 \, dx$

10.  Find: $\int \dfrac{x}{\left(3x^2 - 5\right)^2} \, dx$

CHAPTER 11    Integration

11. Find: $\displaystyle\int \frac{10x^4 + 1}{4x^5 + 2x + 3}\, dx$

12. Find: $\displaystyle\int (2 - 3x)e^{4x-3x^2}\, dx$

13. Find: $\displaystyle\int x\sqrt{x - 9}\, dx$

14. The marginal price for a weekly demand of x bottles of cough medicine in a drugstore is given by:

    $$p'(x) = \frac{-19,350}{(5x + 40)^2}$$

    Find the price-demand equation if the weekly demand is 250 when the price of a bottle of cough medicine is $3. What is the weekly demand when the price is $2.75?

15. A manufacturing company is ready to introduce a new product with a national sales campaign. After extensive test marketing, the market research department estimates that sales (in millions of dollars) will increase at the monthly rate of

    $$S'(t) = 8 - 8e^{-0.3t} \qquad 0 \le t \le 24$$

    t months after the national campaign has started. What will be the total sales 9 months after the beginning of the campaign if we assume zero sales at the beginning of the campaign? (Round answer to the nearest million.)

16. The management of an oil company estimates that oil will be pumped from a producing field at a rate given by

    $$R(t) = \frac{54}{\sqrt{t + 5}} \qquad 0 \le t \le 20$$

    where R(t) is the rate of production in thousands of barrels per year, t years after pumping begins. How many barrels of oil, Q(t), will be produced the first 9 years?

17. If the marginal price dp/dx at x units of demand per week is proportional to the price p, and if at $70 there is no weekly demand [p(0) = 70], and if at $40.18 there is a weekly demand of 10 units [p(10) = 40.18], find the price-demand equation.

18. Given $\int_1^3 f(x)\,dx = 7$ and $\int_1^3 g(x)\,dx = 6$, use properties of definite integrals to evaluate $\int_1^3 [2f(x) - 2g(x)]\,dx$.

19. Evaluate: $\displaystyle\int_{-2}^{1} \left(5x^4 - 2x\right) dx$

## CHAPTER 11    Integration

20.  Evaluate: $\displaystyle\int_1^3 \left(4\sqrt{x} + \frac{1}{x}\right) dx$

21.  Evaluate: $\displaystyle\int_{-0.1}^{0.4} 5e^{3x}\, dx$

22.  Evaluate: $\displaystyle\int_0^2 \frac{6x^2 + 1}{12x^3 + 6x + 3}\, dx$

23.  Evaluate: $\displaystyle\int_{-2}^{46} \frac{x}{\sqrt{x + 3}}\, dx$

24.  A factory discharges pollutants into a large river at a rate that is
     estimated by a water quality control agency to be

     $$P'(t) = t^2\sqrt{2 + t^3} \qquad 0 \le t \le 5$$

     where P(t) is the total number of tons of pollutants discharged into
     the river after t years of operation.  What quantity of pollutants
     will be discharged into the river from the end of the 2nd year to
     the end of the 5th year?

25.  Test marketing for a new health-food snack product in a selected area
     suggests that sales (in thousands of dollars) will increase at a rate
     given by

     $$S'(t) = 20 - 20e^{-0.14t}$$

     t months after an aggressive national advertising campaign is begun.
     Find total sales during the first twelve months of the campaign.

26.  A photocopy shop rents the use of a personal computer and accompanying
     software to the public.  The total accumulated costs C(t) and revenues
     R(t) (in thousands of dollars) generated by the computer satisfy

     $$C'(t) = 3 \text{ and } R'(t) = 14e^{-0.2t}$$

     where t is time in years.  Find the useful life of the computer to
     the nearest tenth of a year, and calculate the total accumulated
     profit during the computer's useful life.

27.  Find the area between the graph of $f(x) = e^{0.5x}$ and the x-axis
     over the interval $1 \le x \le 5$.

28.  Find the area bounded by:
     $f(x) = x^2 - 2x - 15$ and $y = 0$ for $1 \le x \le 4$

29.  Find the area between the graph of $f(x) = 64 - 4x^2$ and the x-axis
     over the interval $[-4, 4]$.

## CHAPTER 11    Integration

30. Find the area bounded by:

    $f(x) = 10 + 4x - x^2$ and $y = 2x + 2$

31. Find the area between the graph of $f(x) = x^2 - 3x$ and the x-axis
    over the interval $-3 \leq x \leq 2$.

32. The income distribution for a certain country is represented by the
    Lorenz curve with equation: $f(x) = \frac{5}{6}x^2 + \frac{1}{6}x$

    (A) Find the coefficient of inequality.
    (B) Use the answer found in (A) to determine if the income of this
        country is (more equally distributed, less equally distributed,
        distributed the same) as a second country having a coefficient
        of inequality of 0.4.

33. Use the rectangle rule to approximate $\int_1^9 \left(4 + x^2\right)dx$ using $n = 4$, and
    $c_k$ as the midpoint of each subinterval.  Compute the approximation to
    three decimal places.

34. Use the table of values below and a Riemann Sum to approximate the
    definite integral.  Use $n = 4$ and choose $c_k$ as the midpoint of
    each interval.

    $\int_0^8 f(x)dx$

    | x | 1 | 3 | 5 | 7 |
    |------|----|----|----|----|
    | f(x) | 81 | 34 | 95 | 94 |

35. The number of cheeseburgers (in thousands) sold each day by a chain
    of restaurants t days after the end of a special sale
    is given by $S(t) = 10 - 8e^{-0.2t}$.  What is the average number of
    cheeseburgers sold each day during the first seven days after the
    end of the special sale?

## CHAPTER 11    Integration

36.  Let $R(t)$ and $C(t)$ represent the total accumulated revenues and costs (in dollars), respectively, for an oil well where $t$ is time in years. The derivatives of $R$ and $C$ over a 3-year period are shown in the graph below.  Use the rectangle rule with $n = 3$ and $c_k$ as the midpoint of each subinterval to approximate the total accumulated profits from the well over this 3-year period.  Estimate necessary function values from the graph.

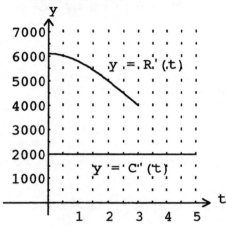

37.  A drug is injected into the bloodstream of a patient through her right arm.  The concentration of the drug, $C(t)$ (in milligrams per cubic centimeter), in the bloodstream of the left arm $t$ hours after the injection is given by:

$$C(t) = \frac{0.11t}{t^2 + 1}$$

What is the average concentration of the drug in the bloodstream of the left arm during the first 5 hours after the injection?

38.  Find the consumers' surplus at a price level of $10 for the price-demand equation:

$$p = D(x) = 30 - \frac{1}{30}x$$

39.  Find the producers' surplus at a price level of $9 for the price-supply equation:

$$p = S(x) = 5 + \frac{1}{1,600}x^2$$

40.  Find the equilibrium price if the price-demand equation is $p = D(x) = 39 - \frac{1}{20}x$, and the price-supply equation is $p = S(x) = 9 + \frac{1}{6,000}x^2$.

## CHAPTER 11    Integration

41.  Find the equilibrium price, and then find the consumers' surplus and producers' surplus for:

$$p = D(x) = 59 - \frac{1}{10}x \quad \text{and} \quad p = S(x) = 26 + \frac{1}{20}x$$

## Key Sheet - CHAPTER 11

[1] $\frac{7}{5}x^5 + x^4 - x + C$

[2] $-\frac{7}{4}x^{12/7} - \frac{1}{2x^4} + C$

[3] $-6\sqrt{x} - 3\sqrt[3]{x^4} + C$

[4] $2e^x + 4\ln|x| + C$

[5] $f(x) = -\frac{8}{3}x^{-3} + \frac{2}{3}$

[6] $P(x) = 80x - 0.08x^2 - 300$
$P(200) = \$12,500$

[7] The advertising campaign should last approximately 38 days.

[8] $p = 130 - 3x$

[9] $\frac{1}{112}\left(4x^7 + 3\right)^4 + C$

[10] $-\frac{1}{6}\left(3x^2 - 5\right)^{-1} + C$
or $\frac{-1}{6\left(3x^2 - 5\right)} + C$

[11] $\frac{1}{2}\ln|4x^5 + 2x + 3| + C$

[12] $\frac{1}{2}e^{4x-3x^2} + C$

[13] $\frac{2}{5}(x - 9)^{5/2} + 6(x - 9)^{3/2} + C$

[14] $p(x) = \frac{3,870}{5x + 40}$; the weekly demand is about 273 bottles when the price is \$2.75.

[15] about \$47 million

[16] About 163 thousand barrels will be produced.

[17] $p(x) = 70e^{-0.06x}$

Key Sheet - CHAPTER 11

[18] 2

[19] 36

[20] $\frac{8}{3}\left(3^{3/2}\right) + \ln 3 - \frac{8}{3} \approx 12.288$

[21] $\frac{5}{3}\left(e^{1.2} - e^{-0.3}\right) \approx 4.299$

[22] $\frac{1}{6}(\ln 111 - \ln 3) \approx 0.602$

[23] 192

[24] $\frac{2}{9}(127^{3/2} - 10^{3/2})$ tons $\approx 311.02$ tons

[25] 123.77 thousand dollars

[26] useful life: 7.7 years
total profit: 31.9 thousand dollars

[27] 21.068

[28] 39

[29] $\frac{1024}{3}$

[30] 36

[31] $\frac{155}{6} \approx 25.83$

[32] (A) 0.28
(B) more equally distributed

[33] 272

[34] $\int_0^8 f(x)dx \approx 608$

[35] 5.69 thousand cheeseburgers

[36] $10,000

[37] 0.036 mg

## Key Sheet - CHAPTER 11

[38] $6,000

[39] $213.33

[40] $24.00

[41] $\bar{p}$ = 37; CS = $2,420; PS = $1,210

## CHAPTER 11    Integration

1.    Find: $\int \left(6x^3 - 4x^2 - 5\right) dx$

2.    Find: $\int \left(4x^{5/7} + \dfrac{1}{x^3}\right) dx$

3.    Find: $\int \left(\dfrac{4}{\sqrt[3]{x^2}} - 2\sqrt{x}\right) dx$

4.    Find: $\int \left(e^x + \dfrac{8}{x}\right) dx$

5.    Find $f(x)$ if $f'(x) = \dfrac{1}{x^4}$ and $f(1) = -4$.

6.    If the marginal profit for producing x units is given by

$P'(x) = 60 - 0.14x \qquad P(0) = -400$

where $P(x)$ is profit in dollars, find the profit function P and the profit on 400 units.

7.    A newspaper is launching a new advertising campaign in order to increase the number of daily subscribers.  The newspaper currently (t = 0) has 24,000 daily subscribers and management expects that number, S(t), to grow at the rate of

$S'(t) = 30t^{3/4}$

subscribers per day, where t is the number of days since the campaign began.  How long should the campaign last if the newspaper wants the number of daily subscribers to grow to 43,000?

8.    The marginal revenue from the sale of compact discs is given by

$R'(x) = 220 - 20x \qquad R(0) = 0$

where $R(x)$ is the revenue in dollars.  Find the price-demand equation.

9.    Find: $\int \left(-3x^2 - 4\right)^4 x \, dx$

10.   Find: $\int \dfrac{x}{(6x^2 + 3)^3} \, dx$

CHAPTER 11    Integration

11.  Find: $\displaystyle\int \frac{4x^3 + 2}{2x^4 + 4x + 5}\, dx$

12.  Find: $\displaystyle\int (4 + 3x)e^{8x+3x^2}\, dx$

13.  Find: $\displaystyle\int x\sqrt{x + 2}\, dx$

14.  The marginal price for a weekly demand of x bottles of cough medicine in a drugstore is given by:

$$p'(x) = \frac{-9,900}{(3x + 75)^2}$$

Find the price-demand equation if the weekly demand is 250 when the price of a bottle of cough medicine is \$4.  What is the weekly demand when the price is \$2.50?

15.  A manufacturing company is ready to introduce a new product with a national sales campaign.  After extensive test marketing, the market research department estimates that sales (in millions of dollars) will increase at the monthly rate of

$$S'(t) = 10 - 10e^{-0.1t} \qquad 0 \le t \le 24$$

t months after the national campaign has started.  What will be the total sales 7 months after the beginning of the campaign if we assume zero sales at the beginning of the campaign?  (Round answer to the nearest million.)

16.  The management of an oil company estimates that oil will be pumped from a producing field at a rate given by

$$R(t) = \frac{35}{\sqrt{t + 7}} \qquad 0 \le t \le 20$$

where R(t) is the rate of production in thousands of barrels per year, t years after pumping begins.  How many barrels of oil, Q(t), will be produced the first 4 years?

17.  If the marginal price dp/dx at x units of demand per week is proportional to the price p, and if at \$80 there is no weekly demand [p(0) = 80], and if at \$60.18 there is a weekly demand of 6 units [p(6) = 60.18], find the price-demand equation.

18.  Given $\displaystyle\int_1^3 f(x)dx = 4$ and $\displaystyle\int_1^3 g(x)dx = 7$, use properties of definite integrals to evaluate $\displaystyle\int_1^3 [-2f(x) - 3g(x)]dx$.

19.  Evaluate: $\displaystyle\int_{-1}^2 \left(3x^2 - 4x\right)dx$

## CHAPTER 11    Integration

20. Evaluate: $\displaystyle\int_1^2 \left(-\sqrt{x} - \frac{5}{x}\right)dx$

21. Evaluate: $\displaystyle\int_0^{0.6} 7e^{3x}\,dx$

22. Evaluate: $\displaystyle\int_0^2 \frac{6x^2 + 1}{12x^3 + 6x + 2}\,dx$

23. Evaluate: $\displaystyle\int_{-4}^{20} \frac{x}{\sqrt{x+5}}\,dx$

24. A factory discharges pollutants into a large river at a rate that is estimated by a water quality control agency to be

    $P'(t) = t^2\sqrt{1 + t^3} \qquad 0 \le t \le 5$

    where P(t) is the total number of tons of pollutants discharged into the river after t years of operation. What quantity of pollutants will be discharged into the river from the end of the 2nd year to the end of the 4th year?

25. Test marketing for a new health-food snack product in a selected area suggests that sales (in thousands of dollars) will increase at a rate given by

    $S'(t) = 40 - 40e^{-0.22t}$

    t months after an aggressive national advertising campaign is begun. Find total sales during the first twelve months of the campaign.

26. A photocopy shop rents the use of a personal computer and accompanying software to the public. The total accumulated costs C(t) and revenues R(t) (in thousands of dollars) generated by the computer satisfy

    $C'(t) = 2$ and $R'(t) = 8e^{-0.3t}$

    where t is time in years. Find the useful life of the computer to the nearest tenth of a year, and calculate the total accumulated profit during the computer's useful life.

27. Find the area between the graph of $f(x) = e^{0.3x} + 1$ and the x-axis over the interval $2 \le x \le 3$.

28. Find the area bounded by:

    $f(x) = x^2 - 2x - 3$ and $y = 0$ for $1 \le x \le 2$

29. Find the area between the graph of $f(x) = 100 - 4x^2$ and the x-axis over the interval $[-5, 5]$.

## CHAPTER 11    Integration

30. Find the area bounded by:
    $f(x) = 6 + 5x - x^2$ and $y = x + 1$

31. Find the area between the graph of $f(x) = x^2 - 2x$ and the x-axis over the interval $-2 \leq x \leq 1$.

32. The income distribution for a certain country is represented by the Lorenz curve with equation: $f(x) = \frac{6}{7}x^2 + \frac{1}{7}x$

    (A) Find the coefficient of inequality.
    (B) Use the answer found in (A) to determine if the income of this country is (more equally distributed, less equally distributed, distributed the same) as a second country having a coefficient of inequality of 0.4.

33. Use the rectangle rule to approximate $\int_{4}^{12} \left(4 + x^3\right) dx$ using $n = 4$, and $c_k$ as the midpoint of each subinterval. Compute the approximation to three decimal places.

34. Use the table of values below and a Riemann Sum to approximate the definite integral. Use $n = 4$ and choose $c_k$ as the midpoint of each interval.

    $\int_{1}^{9} f(x) dx$

    | x | 2 | 4 | 6 | 8 |
    |------|------|------|------|------|
    | f(x) | 87 | 52 | 15 | 63 |

35. The number of cheeseburgers (in thousands) sold each day by a chain of restaurants t days after the beginning of a special sale is given by $S(t) = 8 - 6e^{-0.3t}$. What is the average number of cheeseburgers sold each day during the third seven days of the special sale?

CHAPTER 11    Integration

36. Let $R(t)$ and $C(t)$ represent the total accumulated revenues and costs (in dollars), respectively, for an oil well where t is time in years. The derivatives of R and C over a 5-year period are shown in the graph below. Use the rectangle rule with n = 5 and $c_k$ as the midpoint of each subinterval to approximate the total accumulated profits from the well over this 5-year period. Estimate necessary function values from the graph.

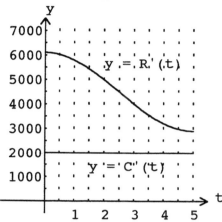

37. A drug is injected into the bloodstream of a patient through her right arm. The concentration of the drug, $C(t)$ (in milligrams per cubic centimeter), in the bloodstream of the left arm t hours after the injection is given by:

$$C(t) = \frac{0.15t}{t^2 + 4}$$

What is the average concentration of the drug in the bloodstream of the left arm during the first 3 hours after the injection?

38. Find the consumers' surplus at a price level of $10 for the price-demand equation:

$$p = D(x) = 20 - \frac{1}{40}x$$

39. Find the producers' surplus at a price level of $10 for the price-supply equation:

$$p = S(x) = 6 + \frac{1}{400}x^2$$

40. Find the equilibrium price if the price-demand equation is $p = D(x) = 46 - \frac{1}{20}x$, and the price-supply equation is $p = S(x) = 6 + \frac{1}{8,000}x^2$.

41.  Find the equilibrium price, and then find the consumers' surplus and
     producers' surplus for:

$$p = D(x) = 55 - \frac{1}{10}x \quad \text{and} \quad p = S(x) = 16 + \frac{1}{20}x$$

[1] $\frac{3}{2}x^4 - \frac{4}{3}x^3 - 5x + C$

[2] $\frac{7}{3}x^{12/7} - \frac{1}{2x^2} + C$

[3] $12\sqrt[3]{x} - \frac{4}{3}\sqrt{x^3} + C$

[4] $e^x + 8\ln|x| + C$

[5] $f(x) = -\frac{1}{3}x^{-3} - \frac{11}{3}$

[6] $P(x) = 60x - 0.07x^2 - 400$
$P(400) = \$12,400$

[7] The advertising campaign should last approximately 55 days.

[8] $p = 220 - 10x$

[9] $-\frac{1}{30}\left(-3x^2 - 4\right)^5 + C$

[10] $-\frac{1}{24}\left(6x^2 + 3\right)^{-2} + C$
or $\frac{-1}{24\left(6x^2 + 3\right)^2} + C$

[11] $\frac{1}{2}\ln|2x^4 + 4x + 5| + C$

[12] $\frac{1}{2}e^{8x+3x^2} + C$

[13] $\frac{2}{5}(x + 2)^{5/2} - \frac{4}{3}(x + 2)^{3/2} + C$

[14] $p(x) = \frac{3,300}{3x + 75}$; the weekly demand is 415 bottles when the price is $2.50.

[15] about $20 million

[16] About 47 thousand barrels will be produced.

[17] $p(x) = 80e^{-0.05x}$

Key Sheet - CHAPTER 11

[18]  -29

[19]  3

[20]  $-\frac{2}{3}\left(2^{3/2}\right) + 5 \ln 2 + \frac{2}{3} \approx -4.685$

[21]  $\frac{7}{3}\left(e^{1.8} - e^{0}\right) \approx 11.783$

[22]  $\frac{1}{6}(\ln 110 - \ln 2) \approx 0.668$

[23]  $\frac{128}{3}$

[24]  $\frac{2}{9}(65^{3/2} - 9^{3/2})$ tons $\approx 110.45$ tons

[25]  311.16 thousand dollars

[26]  useful life: 4.6 years
      total profit: 10.8 thousand dollars

[27]  3.125

[28]  $\frac{11}{3} \approx 3.67$

[29]  $\frac{2000}{3}$

[30]  36

[31]  $\frac{22}{3} \approx 7.33$

[32]  (A) 0.29
      (B) more equally distributed

[33]  5,088

[34]  $\int_{1}^{9} f(x)dx \approx 434$

[35]  7.96 thousand cheeseburgers

[36]  $12,500

[37]  0.029 mg

## Key Sheet – CHAPTER 11

[38] $2,000

[39] $106.67

[40] $26.00

[41] $\overline{p}$ = 29; CS = $3,380; PS = $1,690

## APPENDIX A    Special Topics

1.   Write the first four terms of the sequence $a_n = n[4 + 7(-1)^n]$.

2.   Write $\sum_{k=1}^{4} \frac{k}{4k + 5}$ without summation notation.  Do not evaluate.

3.   Find the general term of a sequence with domain all natural numbers whose first four terms are $\frac{3}{3}, \frac{6}{4}, \frac{9}{5}, \frac{12}{6}$.

4.   Write the alternating series $-\frac{1}{8} + \frac{1}{12} - \frac{1}{16} + \frac{1}{20} - \frac{1}{24}$ using summation notation with the summing index $k$ starting at 0.

5.   Indicate by letter which of the following sequences can be the first three terms of an arithmetic progression and state the common difference for those that are.

     (A) 15, 7, -1, ...     (B) 2, 6, 11, ...     (C) 4, 7, 10, ...

6.   Find the 500th term and the sum of the first 500 terms for the arithmetic progression 5, 9, 13, ...

7.   Find the sum of all the odd integers between 72 and 306.

8.   If a person borrows $12,600 and agrees to repay the loan by paying $300 per month to reduce the loan and 1% of the unpaid balance each month for the use of the money, what is the total cost of the loan over 42 months?

9.   Indicate by letter which of the following sequences can be the first three terms of a geometric progression and state the common ratio for those that are.

     (A) 1, -3, -9, ...     (B) 30, 2, $\frac{2}{15}$, ...     (C) 1, -9, 81, ...

10.  Find the sum of the first 20 terms of the geometric progression 50, 50(1.08), $50(1.08)^2$, ...

11.  Find the common ratio of a geometric progression if the first term is 4 and the 12th term is 25.

12.  Find the sum of the infinite geometric progression (if it exists):

     5, $\frac{5}{8}$, $\frac{5}{64}$, ...

APPENDIX A    Special Topics

13.  Evaluate $C(17,14)$.

14.  Expand $(3x + y)^4$.

15.  Find the sixth term in the expansion of $(a + 2b)^9$.

## Key Sheet - APPENDIX A

[1]  -3, 22, -9, 44

[2]  $\frac{1}{9} + \frac{2}{13} + \frac{3}{17} + \frac{4}{21}$

[3]  $\frac{3n}{n + 2}$

[4]  $\sum\limits_{k=0}^{4} \frac{(-1)^{k+1}}{4(k + 2)}$

[5]  (A) Common difference = -8     (C) Common difference = 3

[6]  $a_{500} = 2{,}001$;     $S_{500} = 501{,}500$

[7]  $S_{117} = 22{,}113$

[8]  \$2,709

[9]  (B) Common ratio = $\frac{1}{15}$     (C) Common ratio = -9

[10] 2,288.10

[11] 1.18

[12] $\frac{40}{7} = 5.7143$

[13] 680

[14] $81x^4 + 108x^3y + 54x^2y^2 + 12xy^3 + y^4$

[15] $4{,}032a^4b^5$

### APPENDIX A    Special Topics

1.  Write the first four terms of the sequence $a_n = n[6 + 7(-1)^n]$.

2.  Write $\sum\limits_{k=1}^{4} \dfrac{k}{5k + 9}$ without summation notation.  Do not evaluate.

3.  Find the general term of a sequence with domain all natural numbers whose first four terms are $\dfrac{5}{2}, \dfrac{10}{3}, \dfrac{15}{4}, \dfrac{20}{5}$.

4.  Write the alternating series $-\dfrac{1}{4} + \dfrac{1}{6} - \dfrac{1}{8} + \dfrac{1}{10} - \dfrac{1}{12}$ using summation notation with the summing index k starting at 0.

5.  Indicate by letter which of the following sequences can be the first three terms of an arithmetic progression and state the common difference for those that are.

    (A) 5, 9, 13, ...    (B) 9, 3, -3, ...    (C) 4, 6, 9, ...

6.  Find the 400th term and the sum of the first 400 terms for the arithmetic progression 8, 11, 14, ...

7.  Find the sum of all the even integers between 53 and 307.

8.  If a person borrows $10,800 and agrees to repay the loan by paying $200 per month to reduce the loan and 1% of the unpaid balance each month for the use of the money, what is the total cost of the loan over 54 months?

9.  Indicate by letter which of the following sequences can be the first three terms of a geometric progression and state the common ratio for those that are.

    (A) 1, -3, -9, ...    (B) 34, 2, $\dfrac{2}{17}$, ...    (C) 1, -3, 9, ...

10. Find the sum of the first 30 terms of the geometric progression 100, 100(1.09), $100(1.09)^2$, ...

11. Find the common ratio of a geometric progression if the first term is 7 and the 12th term is 25.

12. Find the sum of the infinite geometric progression (if it exists):
    $2, \dfrac{2}{7}, \dfrac{2}{49}, \ldots$

## APPENDIX A    Special Topics

13.   Evaluate $C(19,3)$.

14.   Expand $(2x + y)^4$.

15.   Find the fifth term in the expansion of $(p - 2q)^9$.

## Key Sheet - APPENDIX A

[1]  -1, 26, -3, 52

[2]  $\frac{1}{14} + \frac{2}{19} + \frac{3}{24} + \frac{4}{29}$

[3]  $\frac{5n}{n + 1}$

[4]  $\sum_{k=0}^{4} \frac{(-1)^{k+1}}{2(k + 2)}$

[5]  (A) Common difference = 4     (B) Common difference = -6

[6]  $a_{400} = 1,205;$     $S_{400} = 242,600$

[7]  $S_{127} = 22,860$

[8]  $2,970

[9]  (B) Common ratio = $\frac{1}{17}$     (C) Common ratio = -3

[10]  13,630.75

[11]  1.12

[12]  $\frac{7}{3} = 2.3333$

[13]  969

[14]  $16x^4 + 32x^3y + 24x^2y^2 + 8xy^3 + y^4$

[15]  $2,016p^5q^4$

Essentials of College Mathematics, Third Edition
Raymond A. Barnett and Michael R. Ziegler

## APPENDIX A    Special Topics

1.   Write the first four terms of the sequence $a_n = n[7 + 5(-1)^n]$.

2.   Write $\sum\limits_{k=1}^{4} \dfrac{k}{k + 11}$ without summation notation.  Do not evaluate.

3.   Find the general term of a sequence with domain all natural numbers whose first four terms are $\dfrac{4}{3}, \dfrac{8}{4}, \dfrac{12}{5}, \dfrac{16}{6}$.

4.   Write the alternating series $-\dfrac{1}{6} + \dfrac{1}{9} - \dfrac{1}{12} + \dfrac{1}{15} - \dfrac{1}{18}$ using summation notation with the summing index k starting at 0.

5.   Indicate by letter which of the following sequences can be the first three terms of an arithmetic progression and state the common difference for those that are.

     (A) 3, 7, 11, ...    (B) 5, 7, 10, ...    (C) 7, 3, -1, ...

6.   Find the 200th term and the sum of the first 200 terms for the arithmetic progression 6, 10, 14, ...

7.   Find the sum of all the odd integers between 52 and 346.

8.   If a person borrows $19,800 and agrees to repay the loan by paying $300 per month to reduce the loan and 1% of the unpaid balance each month for the use of the money, what is the total cost of the loan over 66 months?

9.   Indicate by letter which of the following sequences can be the first three terms of a geometric progression and state the common ratio for those that are.

     (A) 1, -3, -9, ...    (B) 1, -6, 36, ...    (C) 22, 2, $\dfrac{2}{11}$, ...

10.  Find the sum of the first 25 terms of the geometric progression 200, 200(1.08), $200(1.08)^2$, ...

11.  Find the common ratio of a geometric progression if the first term is 5 and the 10th term is 25.

12.  Find the sum of the infinite geometric progression (if it exists):

     4, $\dfrac{4}{7}, \dfrac{4}{49}$, ...

APPENDIX A    Special Topics

13.  Evaluate C(26,3).

14.  Expand $(x - 2y)^4$.

15.  Find the fourth term in the expansion of $(a - 2b)^{11}$.

## Key Sheet - APPENDIX A

[1]  2, 24, 6, 48

[2]  $\frac{1}{12} + \frac{2}{13} + \frac{3}{14} + \frac{4}{15}$

[3]  $\frac{4n}{n + 2}$

[4]  $\sum\limits_{k=0}^{4} \frac{(-1)^{k+1}}{3(k + 2)}$

[5]  (A) Common difference = 4     (C) Common difference = -4

[6]  $a_{200} = 802$;    $S_{200} = 80,800$

[7]  $S_{147} = 29,253$

[8]  $6,633

[9]  (B) Common ratio = -6    (C) Common ratio = $\frac{1}{11}$

[10]  14,621.19

[11]  1.20

[12]  $\frac{14}{3} = 4.6667$

[13]  2,600

[14]  $x^4 - 8x^3y + 24x^2y^2 - 32xy^3 + 16y^4$

[15]  $-1,320a^8b^3$